Never a Dull Moment
The war diary of Arthur Bloor

Edited by Graham Hassall

Copyright © 2014 Graham Hassall

All rights reserved

ISBN-13: 978-1502869562

ISBN-10: 150286956X

DEDICATION

Thank you to my wife Sarah for supporting the creation of this work and to my sons Evan and Owain for not allowing me to get too immersed in it.

To Eileen for providing my literary education.

To Mum, for eating toast.

To Bill, for a fine example.

Above all, this book is dedicated to the men and women of both sides of this story; may we be always grateful for their sacrifice and learn from their experience.

Armistice

We march with poppies once again,
we march with comrades in the rain.
With boys and girls, who never knew,
the sound of war like me and you.

With Scouts and Guides we form the line,
and march along just one more time,
to church for hymns, we know so well,
and remember in silence those who fell.

Then to the grave of the one who came,
to give his life, but lose his name,
A child, a boy, a mother's son,
who lies in peace, his job well done.

And as we stand, lost in grief,
we remember friends, who lie in peace,
with comrades in a foreign field,
who stood so strong, and would not yield.

They gave their lives, so long ago,
so children now, will never know,
the horror of a full-scale war,
or see the things that those boys saw.

Amen

W.L. Birks

CONTENTS

1	Introduction	Pg vi
2	Leaving England	Pg 10
3	On French Soil	Pg 18
4	The Quick and the Dead	Pg 27
5	White Bread	Pg 32
6	R&R	Pg 38
7	The Parting of Ways	Pg 44
8	Good Germans	Pg 54
9	Into Belgium	Pg 62
10	Take all Risks	Pg 68
11	Epilogue	Pg 77
12	Glossary	Pg 80
13	Gazetteer	Pg 88
14	About the Editor	Pg 89

ACKNOWLEDGMENTS

I take no credit for this work, I have been fortunate only to have the opportunity to edit it. The words are Arthur's supplemented with footnotes and open-source references. Reference and reproduction of both this work and its underlying message for educational purposes, is encouraged and permitted without limitation. All rights in respect to commercial use are reserved.

INTRODUCTION

The Second World War lasted from 1939 until 1945 and involved the vast majority of the world's nations. It was a global and total war, involving some 100 million people; its scale eroded the distinction between the military and civilian populations and necessitated absolute military, economic, scientific and industrial commitment. The causes of the war are complex but were largely founded upon the rise of Nazism in an embittered Germany, still recovering from the harsh and economically crippling peace treaty, following World War I, and the rise of fascism in Japan and Italy. The war eventually formed into two opposing alliances: the Allies[1] and the Axis[2].

Many men left their families to fight for either the Allies or the Axis, leaving behind their families, jobs and homes. This is a personal story of the war written by one of those men: Arthur Bloor, my Grandfather.

Arthur was not a career soldier, rather, like most of the men he served with, he was either conscripted or was a wartime volunteer; although the 'call up' was extended as high as aged 51 as the war progressed, it is likely that on account of his age (37 when leaving for Normandy) and the time of his departure, that Arthur was a volunteer.

Gunner Arthur Norman Bloor enlisted into the Royal Artillery on the 14th August 1941, with according to his medical records, a fresh complexion, and weight of 141 pounds, when he presented for medical at Hanley Medical Board just a short time before.

His military records, very kindly supplied by the Ministry of Defence, show that two days later (16th August 1941) he was at the Combined Operations

---

[1] France, Poland and Great Britain, soon to be joined by the British Commonwealth of Canada, Australia, New Zealand, Newfoundland and South Africa. Both the Soviet Union and the United States joined the alliance in 1941 (June and December respectively) after German aggression upon their own countries.

[2] Germany, Japan and Italy; Russia had an early alliance with Germany but switched sides later in the war.

Training Establishment [HMS Dundonald], Auchengate Camp, Near Troon Scotland. Historic records indicate that only Commando training was conducted at this site during the duration of Arthur's stay, but it is likely, given his enlistment as Gunner, that there was some degree of basic training being conducted also, in order to prepare for the amphibious invasion of mainland Europe.

His records also demonstrate that by the 13/07/42 he had moved on and was at DEAL; Very likely to be Deal in Kent as we know that from January 42 he was with the 2nd Light Anti-Aircraft Regiment, whose services would have been in high demand protecting the capital from aerial attack. Between Deal and Scotland, he has also been in both Deepcut and Yeovil. Whilst at the latter, Arthur was promoted to Lance-Bombardier and later Bombardier but following a course of instruction at the Anti-aircraft school in Sandwich, reverted to Gunner at his own request in August 1942.

At some point, perhaps on account of his [relatively higher] age, Arthur was trained as a specialist, whose role when deployment to Europe eventually came, was to drive, maintain and employ a specialized truck delivering water and rations to the deployed men and guns of his unit. With greater freedom of movement than his peers, Arthur had an insight into the activity of all the sub-units - not at the command level that his superiors would have enjoyed, rather at a human level; it is this insight and his emphatic notes that make his story such compelling reading.

Arthur wrote home regularly we believe, with letters for his wife Olwen, whom he affectionately refers to as Oll, and his children Eileen, Dennis and April, who at the time of his enlistment were aged just 12, 11 and five months respectively. He also however, wrote a series of letters home describing in graphic detail the gruesome events around him. In our modern, super-connected world, it is difficult to appreciate the importance of such communications for men at war for up to five years, and the families they left behind.

In the first of these Arthur specifically asks that the letters be saved until his return, and I believe that from his notes and style of writing, that he had an idea to write his own story at some point after the war was over. It is unfortunate therefore that the story is incomplete, writing as he was around three months after the event, perhaps due to the necessary security censures that all communications were subject to. It is possible that in the final epoch of the war, that Arthur was simply too busy to write, or, that in the excitement of impending victory and return home, that writing in draft seemed pointless. Fortunately we do know some of his movements after his last letter, from the surviving notes that he made along the way and from anecdotal reports from his children.

Arthur's war letters and notes were 're-discovered' by his daughter Eileen at a time when I was recovering from significant injury, and they became a cathartic and consuming project editing them into this body of work. From a personal point of view they served as a valuable insight into the man who I unfortunately never met, he having passed away at the age of 70, just before I was born.

For my part in this project I have contributed little, adding a glossary of military terms, photographs and historic context; the story is all Arthur's and I take no credit for it. Wishing to maintain the gritty authenticity, I have corrected some spelling mistakes and some points of grammar, but only where absolutely necessary to aid clarity; overall the text remains unchanged. This was a difficult decision, but I believe is in line with Arthur's intent. The format is as identical as modern printing methods will allow.

Even as it stands, incomplete, Never a Dull Moment[3] remains an important account of one man's war, serving to remind us of what so many people had to endure so that we might have the freedom we enjoy today. I hope that it gives you as much pleasure to read as it has given me to compile.

Graham Hassall

---

[3] The title makes reference to one of Arthur's comments in Chapter Three.

Above: Arthur Bloor of the Royal Artillery.

CHAPTER ONE
LEAVING ENGLAND

11060057
Gnr A N Bloor.
360 Bty,
B,L,A,
5/10/44

Dear Oll,

This is not an ordinary letter, but an attempt to try and give you some account of my travels since I left old England on route for Normandy.
I want you to save these notes, as I might need them when I get home again.

We left our camp at Battle at 2'30a.m. on Tues the 13/6/44 making for London, where we were to embark. We arrived at West Ham stadium (dog track) in the afternoon, after being feted all the way through the East End.

People were throwing cigs, cakes, toffees and fruit into our trucks as we went along and if we stopped, as we had too many times being in convoy, there was cups of tea for us.

This was the East End and these people realised that we were bound for Normandy and all that it meant at that time. The West End almost ignored us; at best they only gave us supercilious glances.

We parked in the stadium and started work on the vehicles (waterproofing them). My vehicle was a casualty: a loose flywheel due to towing another truck for the last ten miles of the journey. REME[4] had a look at it and decided to indent for a new truck as time was too short to get the repairs done.

We were to sleep under canvas on the stadium pitch while we were waiting for our boat to pull in at the dock; meanwhile there was last minute instructions to be given and special kit to be issued such as lifebelts and emergency 24 hour rations etc.

There was almost a continuous series of shows, concerts and pictures until about 1a.m. but I missed all these as I had to do a lot of running about, handing in my old truck and fetching a new one that I had from Canning Town.

All MT personnel left with their trucks for the docks on Thursday the 15th. We were to wait there for the boat and then help load them aboard.

---

[4] The Corps of Royal Electrical Mechanical Engineers.

All the other chaps were to march down, which they did on the Saturday 17th.

The second night at the stadium was the time when Hitler decided to raid London with the Flying Bombs. That was an experience; nobody knew what they were. They were a secret weapon but we all thought that they were ordinary planes. We could not understand why there was a light on them, but we could see them in the searchlight beams and could see all the ack-ack[5] going up, and when we saw them coming down and heard them explode, we naturally thought that they had been brought down by gunfire. We were cheering and thinking how well the ack-ack gunners were doing; what a mistake. But we got down to bed thinking that they were doing fine.

We arrived at the docks and saw immediately where one had landed (a fair mess), and as the day wore on we saw quite a few of them in the daylight. By this time we knew that this was something new and awful. I saw one drop about 200yds away in a burst of fire and smoke. That was enough and I began to scout around for somewhere to sleep as no boat had arrived. I decided to sleep in a little brick & concrete place that had been built for a fire-watcher's post; it was just big enough for two bunks and I slept soundly that night.

Before I turned in, at about 11a.m. I saw a bomb sailing across the sky. I was not perturbed as I had seen quite a few by this time, but the engine stopped; the light was still on it and it began to dive in my direction, now, I was perturbed! I dived into a shallow ditch and watched this terror approach; the light went out and I waited for the bang, imagine my relief as time passed and nothing happened. I never knew whether or not it was a dud and failed to explode or what, but I was grateful not to hear that bang. The following night I slept with the other chaps in an air raid shelter, it was good and we slept well.

We were doing rotten for food and were buying what we could at an American canteen, as we were not allowed outside the docks.

Saturday the boat arrived and loading started and vehicles were lifted on board and stowed in the holds. It was an 11,000ton vessel; most of the loading was done by evening and the rest of the chaps had arrived too. We could not sail that night so everybody bedded down in the wharf sheds. I slept in the shelter again.

Sunday the 18th we finished loading and we embarked at about 11a.m. Last minute letters were scribbled and posted and we sailed at noon; at last we began to move. Tugs pulled us out of the Albert Dock, through the lock and into the Thames. As we passed down the river we were greeted by a

---

[5] Anti-aircraft fire, derived from the British WWII phonetic alphabet used for voice radio transmissions (AA).

loud speaker from the Ford motor works and they wished us the best of luck.

Later down-stream a sailing barge cut across our path and we collided with it. Everyone was excited except the chap in the barge; very quickly he had his dinghy up and his wife and child in it. Quick work that but he stayed aboard. The river police came on the scene and took the wife and baby onto their motorboat while others tried to tow the barge to the side. They failed and took the bargee off, then the boat sank in a cloud of steam.

After some delay we went on and headed for the open sea. We passed the Thames estuary sea forts and took our place in a long convoy, about fifty vessels.

The journey was absolutely uneventful, so far as we knew: no U-boats[6], no air raids, no nothings; just straight sailing down the Channel. Opposite the Isle of Wight we turned left and made for Normandy, it was now Monday the 19th.

What a sight as we approached the French coast, the sea was simply littered with ships all sorts and sizes. There was a ring of destroyers and cruisers on the outside guarding the invasion fleet as landing operations went on. Our convoy went inside the ring and dropped anchor to wait our turn to go into the beaches to unload. It was magnificent to look around and see hundreds of ships: big capital battleships, cruisers, destroyers, frigates, LSTs, LCTs, ordinary freighters by the hundred and Yankee Ducks, all these milling around and no sign of the Luftwaffe.

Conditions on our boat were pretty bad as it was grossly overcrowded. We did not mind this much as we were only to be on it for a matter of 24hrs (one night), but things didn't turn out that way; the sea got rough and we could not land because of it. We spent six days swinging around the bay, cooped up like chickens when we were all below. Every square inch, every hole and corner was occupied by someone's bed and then there was scores of hammocks slung from the roof which was only 8 or 9 feet high. The whole place looked just like a huge jumble sale with paillasses, blankets, packs, rifles, Sten[7] Guns and clothing etc., all seemingly mixed up; and yet it was all in fairly good order, but what a mess it looked.

Some days the sun shone and it was quite warm but there was too much swell on the sea for us to land. When the sea was really rough it

---

[6] The anglicized version of the German word U-Boot: German military submarines. Although efficient weapons against naval warships, they were most effectively used in economic warfare, enforcing a blockade against shipping carrying military and civilian supplies.

[7] **S**heperd and **T**urpin (**En**field UK) submachine gun.

would swing the boat about so much that it seemed as if it was going over; we could hear the trucks banging on the side down below and we could not walk about without holding on to something. This rolling found the weak stomachs too; first one, then another crawled upstairs to be sick. Others like myself were taking it easy, lying down and trying to sleep, knowing that if we stood up then we should be sick. Most of us were pretty close to it but managed to stave it off by being careful.

Most of the time we were bored stiff, we got fed up with watching the other ships and the beaches. Some spent all their time playing cards for francs; that went on until all the francs were gathered into one pocket then it automatically ceased.

One day, a Flying Fortress came circling around, it was obviously in trouble and seemed to be looking for somewhere to get down. It began to lose height and fire broke out in the wing which broke loose and fell away. Immediately the body of the plane went into a vertical dive and crashed on to the hills just inshore. A tremendous burst of flame went up and that was that. God alone knows what happened to the crew, no one bailed out that I remember.

We took to watching the water as it slid along the sides: countless dead fish floating about killed by mines etc. (we presumed). Then a bundle floated past: it was a British sailor and only God knows how long he had been in the drink. He was long past help and nobody bothered to fish his body out; after all he was only one man and he would sink sometime.

As time passed to the 4th day it became evident the chaps were letting their nerves get on edge. They were getting impatient at being kept offshore; knowing as we all did that the position on the front was serious. We all knew that the troops at the line had had a rough time. They were hard pressed and needed reinforcements so that they could rest, while us, as the necessary reinforcements were all just at sea about two miles offshore, so near and yet so far.

There was several night raids on the shipping but we got no more than bits of ack-ack shrapnel falling on deck. Our reconnaissance unit was not so lucky: their boat got a direct hit and almost the entire unit was lost along with their vehicles and equipment. We saw another body float past, a soldier, no-one bothered.

On Friday the 23rd it was a good calm sea and it pleased everybody, especially when we got word that we were going to land. Two LSTs drew alongside, one on either side of our boat and work started with the derricks lifting vehicles and guns from our holds on to their decks. This went on until about 4p.m. when they pulled away; there was still room for more stuff on them but they had to make the beaches before the tide began to turn at 4'30p.m.

They made it and ran up the beach, then they waited for the tide to ebb and leave them high and dry. They got ashore without even getting the wheels wet. Every vehicle had been prepared to go through four feet of water if necessary.

Myself and vehicle and what others were left, were put aboard two LCTs which are much smaller affairs than LSTs. It was getting late in the evening by the time that we headed for the shore, the tide was very low and the beach authorities would not give permission to land. It was a Yankee boat and as the captain told us this they pulled out to open water again. This was rather depressing to me as it held out the prospect of landing at high tide in the early hours and darkness. Our people laid a smoke screen on the water and that did not help to raise my spirits which were pretty low.

Three of us made a cup of tea in the kitchen and then lay on some forms to sleep. I slept fine and was wakened at 6a.m. it was daylight and we were heading for the beaches. The world looked a much brighter place this morning.

The boat grounded at 7a.m. Sat 24th June and we drove ashore through two feet of water. The vehicle in front of me got stuck in the water almost as soon as he left the ramp. There was just enough room for me to pass so I put my foot down and went splashing on my way.

It was a lovely morning and all was quiet; there was only about six boats unloading at the moment. My truck made it and I kept going till we reached solid ground. We then stopped so that we could carry out the first stage of de-waterproofing on our vehicles. It was at this moment that I first put my feet on the soil of France.

To be continued, *"ah, ah"*. If you are interested, I bet this will be like reading a serial story to you.

    So long Oll, all my love.
    Yours ever, Arth xxxxx

Never a Dull Moment

Above: The Boeing B-17 Flying Fortress: a US four-engine heavy bomber; it was commonly employed in the precision strategic-bombing campaign of World War II, against German industrial and military targets. B17s are estimated to have dropped 640,000 tons of bombs during WWII.

Below: Arthur (middle row, third from left) and troop, in the UK awaiting deployment. Note the 'stripes' on Arthur's right sleeve, an indication that at this time he was a Bombardier.

Above: An LCT, packed to the gunnels with troops, on the approach to the invasion beaches on the 6th June 1944.

Below: *"…I put my foot down and went splashing on my way."*

Above: A Yankee 'Duck' landing stores at the Normandy beaches.

Below: Organised chaos - the Normandy beaches just days after the first landings.

CHAPTER TWO
ON FRENCH SOIL

Same again
10/10/44

Dear Oll,

This is a bit more of the story.

I told you that I had just landed in Normandy. I stopped on hard ground and got out of the truck, then immediately started work on de-waterproofing the truck. Having finished stage one, I had time to look around the beaches as there was a column of Red Cross[8] trucks stationary in front of us.

Everything was comparatively quiet, a few REs. knocking about. They were well dug in, dugouts had good sound covers on them. Several of our knocked out tanks were strewn about, they were amphibious too, and I was surprised to see tanks with propellers on them. There were also a few derelict assault landing craft. Looking out to sea, there was still hundreds of ships. On land, buildings and pill-boxes that had been shattered with gunfire and bombs.

We now got going, there were three of our trucks and we had to contact our Battery HQ. It was comparatively easy because when we had gone about two miles, our Major came along and all we had to do was follow him. We had landed to the east of Arromanches and made our way to Ryes, then about two miles south and there was BHQ. Completed de-waterproofing here then went with our troop who were now going to deploy their guns.

We established Troop HQ at a big farm at Sully; we settled in then I went round sites with water. Afterwards I tested the water in the farm well and decided to fill up from it as it was good water. It was here that I first came into contact with the French people. We bought some cider from them at 5Frs a quart[9]. We did not receive much of a welcome here; they just had to tolerate us.

We bedded down in an upstairs barn, but before we got to sleep we saw a few fireworks: Jerry came over so our chaps began to send some red

---

[8] The International Red Cross is an international humanitarian movement founded to protect human life and health, to ensure respect for all human beings, and to prevent and alleviate human suffering.

[9] Imperial unit of volume equal to a quarter of a gallon or two pints.

streaks through the sky. This was of some interest to us as we had not yet made contact with the real warfare.

It was still 24th of June and our captains now got orders that we were to operate in the future under a new role, this was to be infantry protection and would mean that we were to be detached from our battery and work under infantry orders. It also meant that our guns would be operating right up in the forward areas. This did not please any of us because our guns were not suited for such work, they were too high above ground, they were Morris SP Bofors[10]. Still this made no difference, it was an order and that was all there was to it.

We moved on Sun 25th June to Bruy in order to concentrate with our brigade (129 Brigade). We parked in a field, wide open spaces, dug split trenches because we were ordered to by officers, just dug enough ground out to satisfy them and left it at that. We did not yet know the value of slit trenches; I slept in the lorry that night.

Monday 26th, it rained heavily all day but we made preparations to move in the evening. I did not realise at that time what a nightmare that night was to be.

I was separated from Troop as I was travelling with A Echelon[11]. We set off just as it went dark; we went across fields that were seas of mud and up and down tracks that were the same. We had no idea where we were heading or where we were at the time. We did know that we could hear guns firing and that we were going towards them. We were new troops, never been in real action yet and actual artillery fire was strange to us.

It was well after midnight and we were going across a field that was particularly bad. Vehicles were slipping all over the place and quite a few got stuck in the mud. I was following an anti-tank truck and he lost a little ground on this field, thus making a gap in the column and by the time that we reached the road an MP had allowed several pioneer trucks into the convoy. That did it, it was still raining, pitch black and no driving lights allowed. We arrived at the REs depot at about one o'clock. The sergeant of the depot led us back onto our route and then we had to fend for ourselves.

We went forward a mile or two and asked every sentry we saw if he knew where 129 A Echelon was. We went up and down every track we came to, it was no good, we were in strange country, 2'30a.m., pitch black, didn't know where we were or where to go to and quite a good chance of running into enemy's lines. We gave it up and started to go back from the

---

[10] The 40mm Morris Self-Propelled Bofors Gun.

[11] Tactical grouping of vehicles and stores to replenish and support the forward [fighting] troops.

line a mile or two with the idea of parking till daylight. Just as we pulled up an officer came to us, he knew where we should go to and was going there, so off we went again, him leading on a motorcycle.

We reached Putot En Bassien by the road and then turned off the road across the fields. It was hellish; we had to walk a few yards to make sure that there was no holes or slit trenches and then drive the truck a few yards. Walk, then drive, it was bloody awful and guns banging away all around us. After about a mile of this we arrived, it was still pouring with rain so we pulled up under a tree and just fell fast asleep where we sat.

Someone wakened us at 6'30a.m. and told us we were in the wrong place. We moved two fields up and there was our A Trp HQ, along with A Echelon. We had breakfast and began to take a look around. There was evident signs of battle: buildings bashed about and dead beast lying about in the fields.

The guns were deployed that morning near a village called St Manvieu, our infantry had just driven Jerry out of it, in fact it was not fully cleared yet. I went round the sites in the afternoon, it was bloody horrible; it was my first real contact with actual battle. First a batch of Jerry Teller mines that our REs had lifted and made safe, a dead horse horribly burnt and German kit lying all around the fields. As we drove up a narrow track, we could see a man's leg sticking out of the mud and every vehicle had to go over it. No one bothered, no time, in any case he was past help; more dead at the side of the road and in the fields and then we had to dash along a stretch of road that was under enemy observation.

Came to Norry En Bassin. Bloody awful stink, dead beasts lying about in the hot sun. The village itself was practically destroyed. On towards St Manvieu and two of our guns; they had already been under fire. There had been some bloody fighting here. There was a sharp ridge in the ground as we got down towards the village and German S.S. Grenadiers had defended this very strongly. A Churchill was tipped over on its side (a recovery job), Jerry reconnaissance cars wrecked and dead men strewn all around. Shot in the head, shot in the stomach, in the throat and one of our Scottish Fusiliers had all the flesh from the back of his leg above the knee to his backside ripped away with a grenade. The result was the same for all of them, all dead and going black. It smelt like hell and yet there was a section of infantry about three yards away getting dinner ready. It is surprising what men will put up with so long as they can get a bit of cover.

On through the village, debris practically blocking the road and a dead horse half way across the street. We hurried, it was a bit warm here; turned out of the village towards one of our guns, a bit quieter here. A Bedford truck was still burning here, hit with a Jerry shell. Onto the next gun, this was in a cornfield among our 25pdrs, plenty of noise here and more dead Germans and kit around. Some had been hastily buried and their rifles stuck in the soil with their tin hats on the top almost like scarecrows. I was glad to get back to THQ and tea.

We slept on the ground that night; we were not yet sufficiently battle conscious to realise that on the ground was dangerous and that underground was the thing to be desired. We were to learn soon enough.

Rations were poor and chaps began to scrounge anything that came within reach; a little pig was the first victim, then poultry and potatoes.

After several days our guns were redeployed, a little to the south, facing a place called Cheux (*sher*). It was here that I was able to see some of the strength that the British army had in the field.

Guns of every description were here in apparent confusion but actually they were deployed in good order. There was about 600 artillery guns, 25 pounders, 5.5 guns, anti-tank and Bofors. It was terrific. They were bearing on Cheux and beyond. There was to be a barrage while our tanks pushed through the village followed by infantry. The objective was the river Odon about three miles away.

The following day this was done and our armour was reported to have reached its objective and was pushing beyond the river, but they had by-passed a wood with a few Germans in it. This was to be cleared by infantry. Reconnaissance showed that there was Germans in some strength in this wood with some 88s. These were deadly guns.

Plans were made to attack this wood with infantry giving cover to two bulldozers. These were to push the trees down, so making paths through the woods. The wood was beyond the village so our infantry and Bofors began to move up to the village. A report then came in that Jerry was making a counterattack and that four Tiger Tanks had been seen in the village. A battery of anti-tank 17pdr guns were brought and deployed facing the roads leading from the village. To do this our Bofors had to move across the road into another field.

There was slit trenches (German) everywhere and dead Germans in most of them; one of them was only 18yrs old according to his pay book. What a life, to die for his Fuhrer[12] at that age. There was some gruesome sights, one dead German had no head.

Before our chaps moved across, they were getting dinner ready when one of them picked up a German hand grenade. Of course it was safe, at least he said so; imagine his surprise when he threw it into a trench and *"BANG"* it was not so safe. Lucky for everyone roundabout that it was a deep trench.

The whole troop moved across but did not deploy the guns as we were

---

[12] The self-appointed title (*leader* or *guide*) of Adolf Hitler, the leader of the German Nazi Party and Supreme Commander of the *Wehrmacht*.

waiting to go through the village when it was clear. The officers gave orders for trenches to be dug and everybody began to dig half-heartedly; they were only digging because it was an order, not for their safety. It was here that we were to get our first lesson in battle experience and become battle conscious.

Trenches were about two feet deep when there was a terrific whirring noise, almost a moaning and someone shouted *"All clear"*, it was a joke and no-one moved until our troop commander shouted *"DOWN!"*. Everybody got down but not so quickly as they would on later occasions. *"BANG, BANG, BANG, BANG, BANG, BANG"* it was a salvo from one of Jerry's six barrelled mortars.

It shook everyone up a bit and they lay low for a few moments, then as there was no repeat fire we got up to take stock. What a mess, poor old Fred had got his lot, Ronny and 'Beth' had sustained severe wounds and died in hospital. Cole had only slight wounds and Larky got blast in his eyes; he is now in England recovering his sight or trying too. We buried Freddie there and then, a cross made out of a ration box and his riddled hat as a gravestone.

From then on we realised that trenches were things that counted for most.

The troop now moved about half a mile farther back, out of mortar fire and deployed the guns to wait for a passage through the village.

The following morning several of the chaps were standing against a truck when a shell whistled over. It actually passed between them and hit the truck: *"Bump"*, but no explosion. Lucky for them it was an amour piercing shell and they do not explode. It only knocked a roller off the truck; but it did make us realise that when you hear a shell whistle, then you dive for it and very quickly at that.

I went back to A Echelon which was my proper place; I promptly dug myself a deep trench and covered it pretty thickly with earth.

The troop moved up that day, through Cheux and Trouville to a place called Moen. All these places were just south of Caen and our Div was attempting to drive a spearhead towards Evrecy with the idea of working round towards Caen[13]. There was terrific opposition and our spearhead was submitted to hellish mortar and shellfire.

I went up to take water to the guns, riding with the doors unlatched so that we could jump out quickly if necessary. Wreckage all round, wherever we looked; mud and water and shell holes to an enormous extent:

---

[13] Caen was the main British target for the first day of the battle of Normandy. It proved a tough nut to crack for I Corps and was not finally captured until 9th July 1944, by which time it was completely in ruins and virtually impassable.

motorbikes, cycles, recce cars and Bren Carriers[14] all just pushed off the road and left for recovery to pick up if any of them were worth picking up.

Through Trouville where there were several Jerry field guns that had been knocked out. Then we went like hell for Moen; it was a straight road, about a mile and it was being shelled intermittently.

A Tiger Tank was stuck across the road, knocked out, but I nearly caught a packet because I dodged round it at too high a speed. Still I got past it the right way up so it was OK.

At THQ they had received a lot of mortar fire but the trenches had saved them from casualties.

I went round the sites and they were all well dug in. No casualties but there was plenty of infantry casualties; dead covered with blankets and wounded being taken away on Jeeps fitted with stretchers. RAMC[15] were scouring the woods and carrying them to tracks, where Jeeps picked them up.

As we went to the forward guns we were struck by the stillness of things. No people about, no soldiers, until you took a careful look and then we could see our infantry all showing their tin hats; this was because there was a lot of Jerry snipers at work and they are deadly b------s.

The road to Caen was deserted, dead still; we could see the town and of course Jerry could see us as it was a perfectly straight road. We had a gun down there somewhere on the right so that meant that we must go with the truck. Just as we started some infantry from nowhere stopped us, wanted to know where we were going in that direction. I explained that I had to find a gun that was down that road somewhere. They then explained that there was a wire across the road connected to a chain of mines, they were expecting a counter-attack and were lying in the ditches waiting to operate these mines if necessary. One infantry officer said, if I went over it (the wire) slowly, that it would be alright, another told me to go over it fast and it would be ok. Well, I did it slowly going down, found the gun, detachment were alright, no casualties and then came back over the wire fast. Nothing happened and I was glad to get back. That day, this gun was brought back about three quarters of a mile as it was considered to be too far forward. Then the road was screened by camouflage nets slung across from the house tops to the ground, it took about six nets and they are a fair size.

    Well, so long Oll,
    All my love, Arth.

---

[14] Tracked carrier-vehicle for the Brno Enfield machine gun.

[15] Royal Army Medical Corps.

Above: Arthur's unit were equipped with The 40mm Bofors gun mounted on a Morris chassis. Designed in Sweden, during the 1930's and built under licence by the British, the gun would normally have a crew of six, due to its high rate of fire. It was an effective ant-aircraft gun occasionally used as infantry protection.

Below: The Bren Carrier was a lightly armoured universal platform, upon which the .303in Bren gun (pictured here) was commonly mounted. As well the high mounted featured here, the weapon could be fired from a small aperture on the front, providing optimal protection for the crew.

Above: Tiger I in Northern France, March 1944. This heavy tank weighed over 65 metric tons and carrying 80 rounds of ammunition and was a formidable machine. Thankfully, partly due to the success of Allied bombing, Germany managed to produce no more than 500 before the cessation of the war.

Below: German SS Soldier with a plate shaped pressure-activated, *Teller* anti-tank mine.

"…I was surprised to see tanks with propellers on them…" **Above and below**: the DD Sherman tank showing its twin propellers and with canvas shield erected.

CHAPTER THREE
THE QUICK AND THE DEAD

Same again.

Dear Oll,

Third instalment. I have to scribble these things or I would never get them written, and I want to write them while they are comparatively fresh in my memory.

I came back over the trip wire to the chain of mines. I then went to No 5 Gun; it was on the corner where a track led off the main road into the woods and down to the river Odon. The detachment was still digging in; they needed to as there was quite a bit of intermittent mortar fire.

About three yards from the gun lay four privates of the Wilts, dead and covered with blankets. This gun was ill-fated but no-one knew that at that time. No 6 Gun was up the same track about two hundred yards nearer to the enemy.

I went back to A Echelon and comparative quiet; our own heavy artillery was quite close but we did not mind their noise. I slept in my trench that night as I did every night afterwards for several weeks.

I was getting water from St Gabriel from the river and it was remarkable how peaceful and quiet it was there, and at Coulomb just a few miles back from the line. There was plenty of evidence of battle about though, graves in little groups and singly were dotted along the roadside.

There was 5 of our tanks by the roadside at Putot, all knocked out and burnt up. I also saw about twenty of our tanks outside Brettville L'orguileuse all wrecked; also a Tiger wrecked and completely turned upside down, goodness knows what did that they weigh about 50 ton.

I took water up the next afternoon and found that almost all the chaps were a bit low in spirit as they had endured a night of terrific mortar fire. Thankfully things were much quieter during the day and they were only getting sniped at occasionally that day.

Got back to A Ech and hardly got out of the truck when we had to dive for cover; it was four ME109 Jerry planes flying backwards and forwards, machine-gunning everything in sight. What a bloody horrible noise machine gun bullets make when they are coming towards you. Once in a trench you don't mind them so much.

Fetching water the next day I was travelling towards Norrey when a shell dropped about 20yds in front of us just on the bank side; it didn't hurt anyone so no one bothered and traffic just keeps going.

The church at Norrey was destroyed but there was a memorial to the last war that had not been touched, it was a statue of a French poilu[16] in battle dress with his right hand fully extended and gripping a scroll. It was a bit funny to look at because our signals had used this arm to support their line cables, so there was wires galore all draped from the statues right hand. It seemed as if he was holding these cables so as to help us.

We had still got one of our troop guns deployed in this area (St Manvieu), the balancing spring had been hit with shrapnel and the gun would not elevate properly; it was thus virtually out of action. Still it could shoot at low angles and they had a Bren. We had a couple of casualties here too: Barney (Sgt) got a bit of shrapnel through his foot, not serious, and Taylor got a piece in his arse, his was not too bad.

There was a lot of Jerry tanks & recce cars about the place and our REME got a Jerry Mark 4 tank going in full proper order. Everyone was pleased to see that.

Back in A Ech just getting dinner when "Swish, BANG" and we were well in the trenches before the bang; we could hear the shrapnel swishing through the trees. One dropped direct in a trench in the next field and three of them had 'had it'.

It was now 3rd of July and I took water up to the sites again. It was bloody awful up there. Our Div was driving a spearhead and consequently they were under fire from three sides. Our troop had had a terrible night; every truck had been hit by shrapnel but none of THQ personnel had been hit, they had been low down in their trenches but they had not been able to get any sleep at all. No 4 Gun had been hit with shrapnel, had got a puncture and a burst petrol tank but there was no casualties. No 5 Gun had 'had it' though from a salvo of Jerry's six barrelled mortars. The chaps on guard made a dive under the gun which was dug in about two feet; the fifth mortar bomb hit the gun direct killing the two men and set the gun on fire. It blazed like hell as they were carrying reserve petrol. This along with the petrol that was in the tanks, helped to make the thing an inferno; beside this the heat began to explode the ammo.

How men could have endured such things and still remain sane, beats me. Continual mortar fire, gun blazing, ammo exploding in all directions and the time 12'30a.m. or 0030hrs.

Well they did all that they could do and that was to get away, thank goodness they got away without any further casualties.

This only left our troop with four guns in working order. Our troop commander decided to send No 5 Detachment back to A Echelon to wait

---

[16] An infantry soldier in the French army, especially one who fought in the First World War.

Never a Dull Moment

until they were issued with a new gun. He also sent THQ vehicles back for safety, keeping only the two Jeeps at THQ. Every vehicle had been hit but they were still in running order.

Up till now we had had to deal with mud in abundance, and I really mean abundance; for many days on end it was impossible to travel without skid chains on the wheels. The weather began to improve now, it got quite warm and the sun shone brilliantly. This turned all the mud into dust, and *"oh"* what clouds of dust, it was hard to say which was the worst, mud or dust.

The hot sunshine began to make the dead beast smell. Everywhere dead cows and horses with the occasional pig thrown in, lay about in the most grotesque attitudes. They swell causing their legs to stick in the air, then they keep on swelling until they burst. What a blasted stink, an indescribable stink. Then the flies had got to work and began to multiply, it was a fly's paradise. They became a real nuisance.

One of our officers fell of his motorbike and because only a semi casualty, he came to rest a while at A Ech. We now had about 15 men back in A Ech; originally there was only two of us.

Several of No 5 Detachment were suffering very badly from nerves and as we were being shelled a lot they were very slow at recovering. Incidentally one of the men on No 3 Gun was almost a useless wreck, Just wandering around doing bugger all and no one could do anything with him for almost a fortnight. I was disgusted with him as back in England he was the type who was always ready for a fight; you know the sort, no sooner a word than a blow and yet this detachment had not had to endure anything like the same fire the others had.

We were being repeatedly shelled and occasionally machine gunned by aircraft. This was a game for the quick or the dead. We had to be quick.

There was never a dull moment. One of our planes was coming back from the enemy's lines, obviously in trouble; it burst into flames and crashed into the next field with the usual big bang. The pilot landed by parachute quite close too, walked to the wreckage, looked at it, grinned and made off to HQ.

All dodges were being tried to kill the stink of these dead cattle: soaking them with petrol and burning them, covering them with lime, but it was hopeless until they got bulldozers on the job. Then they began burying them, but of course they could not bury all of them.

I went up again to Troop with water; they were still at Mouen but now along the main road from Trouville to Mouen. It was not a case of speed and getting off that section of road, oh no, Jerry had wrecked several trucks that morning because of speed. Speed meant dust and dust fetches shells and mortars. It was a case of travelling at walking speed, 4 or 5 miles an hour. How difficult that was. To crawl along a good road about 1½ miles long knowing that at any time he might start bobbing a few 'crunchers' over, and us in a truck that could easily do 50 miles an hour. It was a nasty 10 minutes or 20, but it was better than making dust clouds.

We went round sites and THQ; no further casualties but we had to get down while three Jerry planes came over and loosed a few rounds off. THQ had moved back across the road behind a fairly substantial house, this gave them a little added protection from mortar fire.

I was now using 'B Route' to get back to A Ech; it was the correct down route as well as being the shortest. The first time I came down this route we passed what had certainly been a tank battle. There was four Jerry tanks wrecked and two of ours. The RAMC personnel were busy as we went past, burying German dead infantry.

From this scene to Cheux, we went at breakneck speed despite holes in the road or dust, because the road for one mile was under observation of the enemy at Carpiquet aerodrome about three miles away. No time to waste at times like that.

Through Cheux to A Ech. Cheux by this time was a sorry mess; we had shelled it when Jerry was there and now Jerry was shelling it because we were there. That is the way that these things work.

Refugees now began to trickle through the lines, otherwise there were no civilians in the forward areas. They were in poor plight and our chaps were giving their chocolate & sweets to the children as they came past. It was heart-breaking to see but it had to be.

Left: Adolf Hitler; the Austrian-born German politician: the leader of the Nazi Party and dictator of Nazi Germany. Hitler was at the centre of World War II in Europe, and the Holocaust.

Below: *"Cheux by this time was a sorry mess: we had shelled it when Jerry was there and now Jerry was shelling it because we were there. That is the way these things work."*

CHAPTER FOUR
WHITE BREAD

The German opposition on this front (The Caen sector) was certainly quite good and in good strength too. We were making progress but it was slow going, he was fighting all the way.

Our artillery was batting away at him all the time and that means day and night. God alone knows how they endured the continual bombardment but they did do so and held their ground. They must have suffered very heavy casualties but they only retired very slowly. We thought that we were suffering heavy fire but this was nothing to what the Germans had to suffer.

I was up at THQ still at Mouen and had just been getting some spuds from a garden when *"Whizz, Whizz"* and we all dived for it; I must have been slipping or out of practice because I was the last one out of three of us to get in a hole big enough for only two. I squeezed in head first but I could not pull my feet below ground level. I knew they were above the top but I couldn't get them down; it was a case of overcrowding, never have my feet felt so big. It seemed like I had feet as big as houses.

They were mortars, a couple dropped in the field about 60yds away but no one got hit so I gathered my spuds up again and got cracking back to A Ech.

We began at this time to see a bit more air support. It was a pleasure to see our Typhoon planes over Caen and Carpiquet diving in to release their rockets at Jerry's guns and tanks. It was good for morale too, everyone felt better after they had been doing a bit of strafing[17].

The infantry were now across the river and our troop had orders to move their guns across which they did during the night of the 8th of July. It was a fairly quiet night when they moved off, towards Verson (Jerry left Verson the day before), because this route was good road, but as they approached the village they could see a big house blazing furiously, and moreover when they got close to the fire they found the road nicely blocked. This was just what Jerry wanted, a column of guns and vehicles all having to turn round in a rather narrow road and a nice big blaze to light the place up for him.

Well he just started to pile his stuff over, imagine what seemed like chaos in 'hell'. Actually there was no chaos but never have trucks and guns been turned round so quickly. The whole troop got out of that very fortunately without a single casualty.

---

[17] The action of attacking from the air with bullets and rockets.

A detour was made: rough narrow tracks and a narrow bridge over the river without any parapet, but they all got across and took up their positions before first light on the 9th of July.

This place became known as 'Happy Valley', although this was far from a happy place for our chaps.

I went round sites again next day, the chaps were all having a pretty rough time but they were doing their job and morale was much better than it had been for a day or two. They were again in the habit of cracking jokes. It is hardly believable that men can joke under such conditions but it is true, once they got used to being under fire.

Our people were attacking Fontaine L'Eteoupe Pour and we had Bofors Guns well forward. I went round all sites, they were alright, some mortar fire but no casualties. I had difficulty getting to No 2 Gun, on top of a hill; had to go up on a narrow cart track and it was wet and muddy, but the real difficulty was the steepness. It was the steepest hill that I have ever taken a truck up. If it had once stopped moving upwards, it would have slipped backwards much faster than it went up.

The following day the guns were in action against six enemy ME 109s that came flying low along the hilltop. No 1 Gun could not open fire because the targets were out of their field of fire due to some tall trees being behind their gun. No 6 Gun opened fire and followed the targets with shells all along the ridge. As the planes flew along they passed behind the trees that were against No 1 Gun, a shell from No 6 hit the trees, exploded and shrapnel hit three of No 1 Gun crew. Two of them were only slightly injured but poor Paddy got it. A bit of shrapnel as big as half a crown went through his tin hat and got stuck in his head, he is now in England, well in health but we believe he has lost his reason.

At this time we only had four guns in action, No 5 Gun was completely destroyed and No 3 could not elevate at all so both these detachments along with No 3 Gun were with us in A Ech.

The third day in Happy Valley I took Taffy Thomas (out of Three Detachment) up to Troop and round sites with me. Going up was quiet but round sites was different; we had to jump in trenches at two sites because of mortars. Well when we were travelling between sites we could not hear them coming because of the noise of the engine etc. so we just couldn't take cover, just keep going. Taffy didn't like this and he said "------- *you, I'm not coming round with water again!*" Of course he would have done if it had been necessary.

We had bread issued at this time (11th July), real white bread, it was the first bread we had had since we left England. Two half slices each and it was almost like cake to us; there was not a crumb wasted. Furthermore we had been promised another issue for the next week. Never had we realised how precious bread was until we had lived for over a month on hard biscuits.

On the 12th A Ech moved up, in fact events proved too far up and they had to move back again. There was a lot of this poor organizing going on; already A Ech had twice moved up, too far forward and had to go back again.

This time (12th July) we moved up to the main Caen Villers Bocage main road. Our section (A Trp) was about 200yds over the road in a field that was about three feet lower than the next field; this was important as cover.

We immediately began to dig in along the edges, under the cover of the next field. It feels good to have three feet of earth between us and Jerry with his mortars and shells. We dug trenches and covered them with anything we could find, then settled down for the night. He shelled us all night through.

I was on guard from 1a.m. until 2a.m. but we couldn't get out of the trenches for more than a few minutes at a time. There came plenty over but no direct hits; close enough to make us get down as far as possible.

At 2a.m. I crawled over to the next trench to waken Taffy Thomas and Jack Robinson; they were next on 'stag'[18]. I wakened them, gave them the watch and they said drowsily *"OK"*. I went back to my trench, three yards away and was getting in as a shell whistled. I dived to the bottom; it still whistled and I almost tried to push myself into the earth. Instead of this shell giving a whistle and then a bang when it went off in the field, it whistled louder and louder. I thought this one was mine. "BANG", some bang it was; I thanked God it never touched me. It was all in a second or so but it seemed like an age, listening to that screaming whistle getting louder and louder until the bang. When the daylight came we found the hole about six feet away from Taffy's trench. I bet that really wakened them up.

One of the boys in a trench further up was absolutely broken up. He was in No 5 Detachment and his nerves were just steadying up a bit after the 'do' when their gun was hit. This heavy shellfire made him crack again. He cried like a baby and had to be held down. Poor Roy, he got killed later in another 'do'.

It was bloody awful about this time; I began to think whether or not I should go mad. Everybody and everything round about was mad, I swear.

When we moved up in the afternoon, we had not got enough room on the trucks for all the kit so we left a sergeant and two gunners to be fetched up later. As darkness came on a DR came in to tell our officers that one of the gunners was dead and the other was almost. It seemed that we were running into trouble wherever we went. Inquiry proved that one of them

---

[18] A colloquial term referring to sentry duty. E.g. to be *"on stag"*.

found a German 37 millimetre shell; the sergeant said *"Throw that ------ thing away"*, instead he gave it to Wilcox saying *"Look at this, it's safe enough"*, Wilcox took it in his right hand and tapped it on the palm of his left hand. That was his lot. Lexton suffered severe injuries and we thought that he too had 'had it'. The muscle of his arm was ripped away, terrible flesh wound in his thigh, foot wound, face wounds, a broken jaw and a bit of shrapnel right through his cheek, but amazing as it may seem he is now in England making a splendid recovery. Wilcox was buried and another wooden cross decorates the soil of Normandy.

Morning came and besides the strafing there was no casualties among the personnel; but some trucks had suffered and the decision was made to move back. Now an argument set in between the officers concerned. It was obvious that Jerry was shelling the road and we were getting the fringe of his fire. We could lie in our trenches as shells whistled over and watch them explode on the roadside 200yds away. One officer wanted to move back to the other side of the road (that was absurd), and the other officer wanted to go back where we came from. The day wore on but we moved back to our original site late in the afternoon.

I took water along that road to the sites that same morning and I was glad to get back thanking God for a safe return.

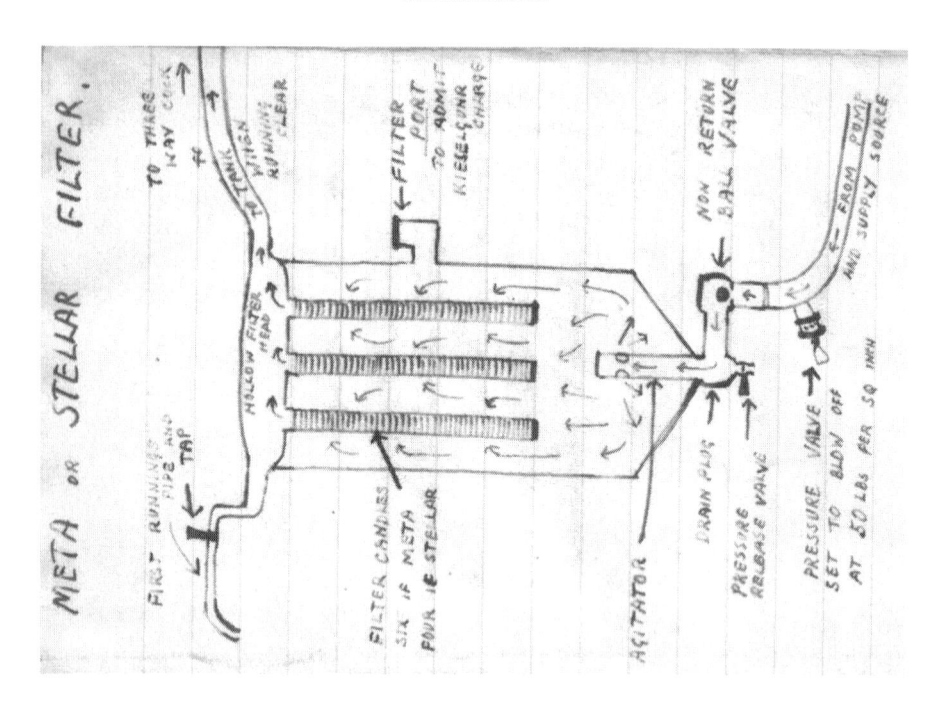

Above and below: Extracts from Arthur's notebook: the water filter which he was equipped with and guidance upon where to find water and wells.

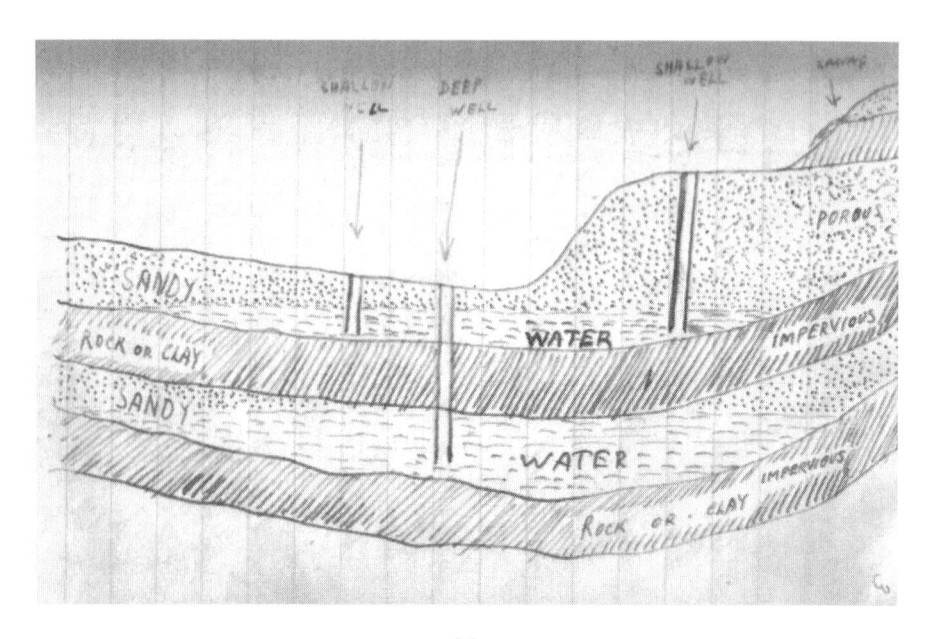

Above: Arthur stands proud next to the Wyvern [emblem] of his 43 (w) Inf Div (part of 30 Corps).

CHAPTER FIVE
R&R

Dear Oll, Same again

The 28th of July and as I told you, we arrived at Lt Leger for seven or ten days rest. We did not know which it was to be but we were hoping that it would be ten. We had certainly earned it; other Divs had been in the line after us and yet they had been rested before us.

We had spent over a month on one of the stiffest battlefronts ever; the Caen battlefront will or ought to be remembered as one of the most terrific fights ever staged. We, the 43rd Div had, had the job of driving a spearhead into the middle of tremendously strong forces; we had faced and battled with the famous SS Troops[19] and Panzer Grenadiers[20].

Only those who have met the SS can tell you how they fight. They do not surrender, they fight until they get killed and they have to be killed. They dig themselves into a foxhole with no hope of getting out to retreat and keep on shooting until they get killed. I saw one with his legs practically burnt away from the knees down to his boots. I don't know how that happened but there it was.

We were told about one that had dug in on Carpiquet aerodrome and our chaps could not shift him until several of the infantry crept near enough to lob four hand grenades into his trench. Even then, he threw three of these out and the fourth one blew his arm off as he was just throwing it back; that left him as easy meat.

His snipers were different and a dammed nuisance, they had special camouflage suits and used to hide themselves, fire all their ammo then walk out with their hands up. Our chaps did not like taking a man as prisoner after he had probably shot several of their pals in the back. They come out with their hands up, expecting to be taken as prisoner but I am afraid that some of them suffered a severe disappointment. Sometimes they would dress as civvies, shooting at night and walking about the villages in the day.

About the time we were around Cheux we were told that some of the

---

[19] The *Schutzstaffel*: a major paramilitary organization under Adolf Hitler. The SS grew from humble beginnings as Hitler's personal bodyguards, to be one of the most powerful and feared organizations of the Third Reich and was responsible for many war crimes.

[20] German mechanized infantry.

enemy soldiers were deliberately colouring their faces yellowish and lying by the roadside as if they were wounded. Their job was to wait for some of our men to advance past them and then they were to open fire and kill as many as possible. Our instructions from then on were to shoot at any German body we saw lying by the side of the road. If it was really a dead Jerry then it was one bullet wasted and if it was otherwise, then it was a bullet well spent.

All this had turned us into experienced and battle wise soldiers and believe me, it makes a difference. We had learned a lot; at every new location we immediately orientated ourselves, finding north, south, east and west, thereby knowing the direction that enemy shells would come from, even before any did come. We always looked for cover and made some as soon as possible. We learned to keep our vehicles in tracks of previous vehicles as much as possible, not to let the wheels go on the verges because of mines; nasty things mines. When the REs had tested a road it was OK, but until then it was a case of being careful. Breaking new tracks across fields etc. was always a ticklish business.

Now all that was past and done with for a few days at least. We read in the papers about men coming out of the line having nice hot baths and going rowing and all sorts of things but we never got round to anything like that. There was a few concerts and picture shows. I managed one concert, George Formby with his wife Beryl and they were real good.

Most of the chaps were more interested in getting to Bayeux. Troop had undertaken to run one liberty truck each evening and that meant about 20 each night so it was a case of taking turns. It was understood that there was three brothels open in the town and a lot of the chaps were eager to get going. 20 men were detailed for the first evening and everyone else had to wait of course.

We got down to business, fixed ourselves up with bivouacs, above ground, then set to work cleaning the trucks and guns, doing all the minor repairs that were necessary.

We were by the side of a river so I parked my truck right on the riverbank and camouflaged up. This enabled us to get water for the troop without moving the truck at all.

I remember that evening when the liberty truck arrived back, twenty people went out with smiling faces and great expectations; twenty faces arrived back full of disappointment. First all the brothels had been closed and there was an MP on them to see that no British troops went in them. Second, there was no beer; that was nasty. Third, there was no grub to be had; in fact there was sweet Fanny Adams in the place except butter (4/-lb), and Gruyere cheese. Some of them bought cheese just for the sake of spending money.

I went there on the second night and the only place of interest was the cathedral; never has there been so many soldiers in a cathedral. The town was packed with troops and devoid of interest except for the cathedral, so eventually they all found their way to it and stood around in crowds. It was worth seeing though, lots of things attracted small crowds of soldiers. There was a copy of the Bayeux Tapestry there, it depicts the story of William the Conqueror invading England.

We managed to find a café where we got some supper, worth about a tanner[21] in England; you would not for shame to put it on the table at home, but they charged us 35 francs (3/6), bloody swindle. No one had any desire to go into Bayeux a second time.

Several of us managed to do a bit of swimming in the river. It was not really deep enough at first but we soon deepened it by throwing a few grenades into it.

I went to the concert and I enjoyed that, then on the third day we had orders to prepare to move! That knocked us flat; we were looking forward to several days of ease as we had just about finished all our jobs up, then we got this order and were told that we should probably move next morning, as we did.

There was air raids each night and a lot of ack-ack but nothing to trouble us.

We packed up and the recce[22] party left at 5a.m. the next morning (August 1st) (not sure of these dates, it was on a Saturday). We were told the same morning as we were waiting to move off, how things were. The enemy were showing signs of trying to disengage and therefore that we (the 2nd Army), had got to put everything possible into the attack, to take full advantage of the enemy's weakening position. I believe that I wrote and told you, just before we left the Caen Sector that there were signs of him beginning to move.

We moved to a concentration area and then took to the road about 2'30 in the afternoon. Our guns were dispersed amongst the infantry; as their job was infantry protection. This meant THQ travelled as a separate unit with the guns at long intervals in the column.

Our destination was a place called Livry which was close to Caument, south of Bayuex. We should have been in the same field as the Anti-tank HQ. We arrived in the new area about half hour after midnight. It was now Sunday, we were all tired and could not locate the ATHQ, and enemy shells were coming over intermittently.

Troop Commander decided to park where we were until daylight. We

---

[21] Informal and historical term for a sixpence.

[22] Military abbreviation for reconnaissance, the act of exploring beyond the forward line of own troops.

pulled into the field and started to dig in. Nice job that, digging a trench in the dark; we had to do it though. I dug one just big enough to let me lay full length and about two foot deep. I got down to sleep at about 2a.m. All this time, our guns were banging away over our heads (we like that), and a few enemy shells kept coming back to us (we do not like them).

At approx. four o'clock I was awakened by a tremendous earth tremor; it was an enemy bomb that dropped into the next field. It hit an ammunition truck and set it on fire. That made a hell of a row, as well as a fireworks show; I could see the stuff going up in the air as I lay in the trench. It was no real danger to us so we just turned over and went off to sleep again.

We got up at 6'30a.m. as our officer had located the anti-tank people and got ready to move again, they were only about 300yds away.

A lot of our four-engined bombers began to go over at about seven o'clock and it amused us to watch them go over and drop their 'eggs'. We moved across about four fields and began to dig in again. We could not help watching the bombers doing their stuff. Occasionally they would drop a big one; we watched it go down and then watched the blast go up. It goes up in rings like the rings in a pool when you drop a stone in it. It was good to watch.

While we were digging in, our officer went out and located our guns. I went round with water and while at No 4 site we had to take cover as a sniper started work and wounded a couple of infantry wallahs[23]. He did not last many minutes and all was quiet again.

Our infantry went into the attack the following afternoon and all our guns moved forward with them. Our Tp Com decided to move a skeleton THQ forward and leave all the vehicles behind that he could; they were to follow the next day. This meant that we had to move again; only one field, but we were only a small party now and we had to move for safety and join some other units that had been left behind. This meant digging in again.

Our Tp Com took a sergeant with him to the new THQ and his job was to come back to us and show us the road up on the following day. When they established THQ several of them went on the scrounge and tried to enter an empty, or rather a deserted house with all the furniture etc. still there. Dick was just going to push the door open (it was ajar) when our sergeant shouted and stopped him. That shout saved Dick's life; the house was booby-trapped all through. Wires across the steps and windows, wires connected to every door and a nice big mine inside all ready to go off. They beat a strategic withdrawal.

---

[23] Of Indian origin, meaning a person of specified kind or role; it was a widely used military term at this time.

They did find a bottle of Calvados though and of course they got into it. Our sergeant got drunk, yet he rode a motorbike all the way back to where we were bivouacked. He will never know how he did it. He arrived back at dusk and gleefully pulled two full bottles of the wicked stuff out of his pockets. It is like water to look at but what a kick. Within five minutes our cook was absolutely blotto. I did not know that men could get drunk so quickly. We all had a share but most of us took it easy. Mind you we had too much because it is so hellish strong. It was a damn good job that no enemy patrols got through that night; we should have been easy meat.

I was on guard from 12 till 1a.m; Tamplin and Stuart sat up with me because I had collared the bottle and was dishing it out in small quantities. It drizzled with rain and by 1a.m. I was fuzzled and slipped down into my trench and slept like a log. Stuart went to bed but Tamp stayed up with the next guard. He was real drunk. He went to bed at 2a.m. took his boots off and got out of his trench for a 'piss' before going asleep. He got out but could not find his way back. He crawled round that field till nearly 3a.m. without any boots on in the wet grass. The chap that was coming on guard at 3a.m. (he was sober) located him and put him in his trench.

The next morning he came up for breakfast without his boots and we had to search the field for them; they were in the grass, yards away from his trench.

This day, us that were left behind received orders to join A Ech. We did this and of course we had to dig in again.

I went up to Troop and sites, they were just south of Caumont. There were a lot of minefields in this area. The Royal Engineers got to work and taped them off but we still had to be careful. There was holes all along the side of the road where mines had gone up and quite a few of our vehicles too.

Above: Another of Arthur's newspaper cuttings. Marked '*Save this*', it depicts the ruined Caumont where much heavy fighting took place.

Left: One of the biggest and most famous performers of the time, George Formby meets troops in France, along with his signature ukulele. Formby worked extensively for the Entertainments National Service Association (ENSA), and entertained as many as three million service personnel.

CHAPTER SIX
THE PARTING OF WAYS

Same again
30/10/44

Dear Oll,

There is one incident that I ought to have written earlier: When the troop were up at Mouen and I was in A Ech just outside Cheux, I went to draw some water at Brettville L'Orgeileuse. I only got water at this place twice because it was not an abundant supply. We had to get it out of a well in the main street and there was several water trucks before me so we settled down to wait.

Now this place was well behind the line and all the troops there were either back-line boys or new troops coming up, ready to go into the line. I mention this to show you that all these chaps were not battle conscious but Sandy and I coming from the line were only too conscious.

Well I was talking to two schoolboys and Sandy was about three yards away talking to a Scottish Fusilier, when the familiar whistle of a shell put both of us on the ground in very quick time. There was no bang though and as we got up, we could see that we were the only ones that went down and everybody wanted to know what was going on. It must have been a vehicle that made the whistle but me and Sandy went down automatically; we laughed like hell after we got up but I hate to think what would have happened to all those other chaps if it had been a shell.

To get back to the proper sequence, Troop was up beyond Caumont in a farmyard where they found the Calvados. Joe Whitear went up with me and while I went round sites he went on the scrounge. He came back with six chickens; he killed them and left three with troop. We took three back with us to 'Ech', they made a grand dinner the next day.

We went up again the following day and troop had moved forward again; they were now in the grounds of a big chateau about half way between Cahagnes and Sept Vents. The guns were dispersed with the infantry and we had difficulty in finding them. One of our sergeants about this time began to have trouble with his nerves, (I cannot blame him) he applied for reversion to the rank of Gunner and a transfer to the REs. He got his reversion but not his transfer. He had been ordered to take his gun forward and had failed to do so, as he thought that the position was too far forward. It was put down to loss of nerve and he was reverted to Gunner.

I was taking the truck along a track on the way to one of our guns when a sentry stopped us; we only had to wait while they blew a tall tree down. It was in the way of a 25pdr so they just gave it a charge of TNT[24].

There was a pretty heavy raid on our forward areas that night; a lot of flares and tracer and all that. Some fairly hefty bombs too, close enough but not too close to cause any casualties in our troop. It is a peculiar thing that no-one seemed to bother at all about bombs dropping, they do not affect your nerves like shells do.

We were here for two days and then moved forward again. Things were moving on this front a bit faster than they had done on the Caen Sector. This time our guns were deploying around the village of St Purre Le Tresne. Two guns were in the edge of the Bois Du Homme which is a great big wood, and I was warned not to go too close to the brow of the hill as it was under direct observation of the enemy who was yet, close too.

There was a hell of a mess around here, the usual stinking dead cattle and horses, wrecked lorries, guns, Bren Carriers & tanks. The road had been blasted by our own aircraft with bombs and it was almost impossible to traverse it, zig-zagging round bomb craters and up and down loads of earth and stones that the bomb had thrown up. There was a great big Jerry Ferdinand Tank stuck on the crossroads that our infantry had knocked out with a PIAT[25], and at the little village school, there was about a dozen Jerry rifles stacked against the wall, the owners having been taken prisoner.

We were now warned again to keep to cover and not even show our drinking mugs, as they were white.

THQ was in a wrecked farmhouse; there was bags of cider here and I took a couple of bottles back with me. This place had been wrecked from the inside by a booby trap. Our REs exploded it so no one was hurt; they make a hell of a mess.

A Ech moved up this day to some fields quite close to where our THQ had been in the chateau grounds. We dug in again and got settled.

Went to troop again the next day but could not find either THQ or any of the guns. We tried every road that we could see but it was no use until we met one of our DRs; he took us along a winding track to a little village (forgotten the name) where we found THQ in an orchard. The troop sergeant took us round to the guns and to my surprise they were all hidden in the woods, not deployed but packed up ready to move at half an hour's notice. They were waiting for the infantry to give the word when they were ready to make the attack. They were Guns No 1, 2, 3 & 4. No 6 had to move forward, but did so that same evening. No 5 had not yet been

---

[24] Trinitrotoluene, an explosive compound. The name however is often used to refer to any type of explosive.

[25] British anti-tank weapon: Projector Infantry Anti-tank.

replaced.

The sites had been under heavy shellfire the night before but got no direct hits and therefore no casualties. A truck load of ammunition had been hit on the road and the stuff exploding in it had just ripped the whole thing to bits; it was scattered all round in all bits and tatters.

There was a young cow hobbling about the field where we were in A Ech; it had been hit in the foot by some shrapnel. There was no farmers or anyone about to do anything for it so we decided that the best thing to do was to make good meat out of it. We rounded it up and Joe the butcher tied it to a tree. McMaster got his Sten Gun and Joe told him where to put the bullets. Mac put his gun to the cow's head then 'CRACK, CRACK' and down he went. Joe goes in with a knife and off comes the cow's head. I think he worked for about an hour and then we had a good stock of meat.

We took some up to THQ the next day and round the guns as well. No 1, 2, 3 & 4 Guns were still waiting for the infantry, but No 6 had moved well forward almost to the top of the hill.

We passed a Tiger with his 'teeth drawn' on the way up. That is how we like to see the Tiger Tanks; their 88 millimetre gun is a deadly weapon.

I was getting water now at a small stream outside Cahagnes. This place was completely wrecked. Water supplies were not too good hereabouts but I was managing alright.

We knew that something big was coming off as our guns had been kept hidden for 34hrs, but we did not know what was to be the objective. We were to know soon enough.

At about this time the 'Yanks' were beginning to push out to the south and we were exerting a lot of pressure on the enemy to keep him engaged and thus prevent him moving any of his amour and infantry to the south.

We were about seven or eight miles short of Mont Pincon and this was our objective although we did not know it at this time.

Our infantry moved into the attack in the evening and our guns and all supporting arms moved forward in column as the infantry cleared the ground. The idea was to move forward enough to deploy all supporting arms within range of the '*Mont*' (mountain). Our guns were dispersed again among the infantry and THQ was in the brigade column. They moved into Lurgues at dusk; Jerry had only just left and the place was still on fire. This was another village that was wrecked as the war moved on. Jerry had fired most of the buildings before he left.

A Tiger had got stuck in a ditch and leaning against a house. It could not move, so the people were told to get out and set fire to the tank. This of course also burnt the house down.

The column moved through Lurgues; St Mesnil Azouf had not suffered too badly. Early next morning our brigade moved back to St Mesnil and then struck east, direct to Mont Pincon. Our troop guns were deployed around the base of Mont Pincon and THQ was at Duval, that also was close to Mont Pincon.

We went up from A Ech to find troop and could not find them anywhere; we did not know that they were at Duval. We came back and went to Battery HQ but they could not tell us where they were. In the afternoon A Ech including us moved to the Bois Du Homme, just beyond St Pierre. He shelled us fairly heavily here but it did not worry us much because they were pitching about 200yds over us. When we got used to them 200yds seems a long way.

After we had dug in we went up again to find troop, but it was no use; we found Brigade HQ but even they could not give us Troop's location. Brigade was in St Mesnil but they were preparing to move again. Everybody was on the move and we were all out of touch. We went back, had tea and then got orders to move again. This was the second move on this day and we had dug in there for nothing, but there it was.

We were getting worried about Troop because it was getting late in the day and they would be waiting for water and rations. We moved forward through St Mesnil Azouf to about half way from St Mesnil to Duval. Got there at nearly 9p.m. and then immediately set out again to try and find Troop.

We found X troop; they were in our battery and they were able to give us an idea where A Trp was. We found them at 9'30p.m. and gave them the rations and water, then went back again to our location to start digging in again. This was a war of picks and shovels at this time.

I had to go back for water the next day and saw quite a lot of wreckage on the road: tanks, armoured cars, recce cars, and Bren Carriers etc. There was a tank (Jerry) at the side of the road with the gun barrel sticking across the road, so our REs put a charge in it and blew it off. A Sherman Tank was at the roadside with only one hole in the turret, but that was enough; an 88 shell had gone through that turret as if it was paper and it must have ricocheted all-round the inside because all the crew were still there, dead of course. They could not be got out because when they go into action they lock themselves in. We could see them through the portholes; I suppose someone would get them out sometime, their bodies were beginning to smell rather badly.

There was a few dead Germans in the ditches and there was one of Jerry's recce cars at the side of the road completely burnt up, with the driver still at the wheel. He was just a cinder of a man now; we could just recognize the shape of a man, but now he was only the size of a boy.

I went up to Troop again and they had had a hell of a time. No 6 was not too bad but No 4 was under observation of the enemy on the mountain and they were being punished very badly. Every time a man moved out of cover Jerry would send a salvo of mortars over. Three of the four wheels had already been punctured and it was only the trenches that saved the men.

The bad sighting of our guns was due to our guns being put under the direction of infantry officers, who knew nothing about the sighting of guns. They sighted this gun during the night not realizing that daylight would expose it to observation.

Our troop commander had withdrawn No 1 and 2 to THQ, and No 3 had to come in later as it was again put out of action by enemy fire.

I went back to A Ech with orders that we were to leave A Ech and go to our BHQ. We moved there immediately; it was at St Mesnil. Dug in again.

Ten minutes after I had left THQ they were shelled again and three of the chaps got hit, all in the legs. Two of them were fairly bad, all three of them went back to England.

That night Jerry counter-attacked and No 4 Detachment had to leave their gun; they could not move it so they took the breechblock out and buried it. The infantry were falling back so the detachment came back to THQ. They had had a hell of a time but no casualties. It was incredible.

The following morning the brigadier played hell with our troop commander for withdrawing the guns and ordered him to put them out again. He was too late though; by this time we had only got two guns that were fit for action: No 5 still not replaced, No 4 was in enemy hands and No 3 and No 2 had been hit with shrapnel and could not be put into action. These two guns and detachments along with No 4 Detachment came back to BHQ so that the guns could be replaced.

Every gunner in Four Detachment was showing signs of distress. All dirty and unshaven and badly in need of sleep; their nerves were in a very bad state. Only rest could put them right and they needed grub. Practically all their kit had been left on the gun limber, so blankets were fetched from B Ech[26] and dished out; they were fed and all got down to sleep. 'Wakey' tried to tell me what a time he had, but was in a bad way himself so I told him to get some sleep and tell me afterwards.

Our infantry regained the lost ground again that day and No 4 was still there. That was a surprise as we thought that Jerry would have set fire to it. The limber had gone though with the men's equipment. Three new wheels were taken up and fixed on, the breechblock was replaced and the gun brought out again.

Jerry by this time had been driven farther back and our infantry was on top of the hill. They had a hell of a time in this job and suffered very heavy casualties. This was the highest hill in Normandy and had to be approached

---

[26] Second-line support and administrative grouping.

by a steep winding road; at the bottom the road went over a small bridge and wound round a lake then up a steep climb. The commanding officer of the Fourth Wilts got his 'lot' on this bridge and the ambulances were kept very busy.

We had six tanks helping our infantry and the job was done; the hill was in our hands but it had been a real bloody fight.

Our brigade was now withdrawn to refit for four days. Our troop and L Troop went right back to the chateau near Sept Vents. We could not understand this but we were not left too long in ignorance. Our troop commander told us that A Trp and X Trp were going to be disbanded and surplus personnel were to be used to reinforce the infantry, to help make good some of their casualties. He told us that this was to be the last day of A Troop. Fourteen of us were to be transferred to L Troop to replace fourteen of their personnel who would then be surplus. Well, none of us liked the prospect of things to come at this time. It was the parting of ways for a lot of men who had become good friends and been through a lot of enemy fire together. The majority of us had been in A Trp since it was formed in Feb 1942.

We erected bivvies and handed over the guns. I was to take my truck with me to L Troop so I had no trouble. We were going to sleep on the ground as this place was now well behind the line and out of range of shells. There was a small barrel of beer that had been issued to troop but had not been dished out because we had not had time up till now. We all decided to make a day or rather a night of it. First one and then another brought out a bottle of Calvados and Cognac; one officer produced a bottle of Gin. Well we polished the beer off first and got down on the grass and started on the spirits, all neat. What a night. Everyone was friends; everyone was drinking and there was any amount to drink. Of course everyone got blind drunk, really drunk. Gunners, Bombardiers, Sergeants and officers all drunk and jolly good luck to them all. They had well earned a good booze up and we had one.

We all fell out of circulation as we lost consciousness. One of the sergeants went to slap someone on the back, you know, just a hearty slap on the shoulders. He missed his aim and went full length flat out; no one bothered, he crawled to his bed later on. Jack Robertson tried to get to his bivvy[27] while he still had the use of his legs; he reached the bivvy but the entrance was a different matter, it would not keep still and it took about a dozen tries to get through it. His legs kept taking him past it. Bdr Bridger kept on taking it until he just went down where he was and that was his bed for the night. He was there the next morning. Jim Scott crawled away on all

---

[27] Bivouac: a temporary improvised encampment.

fours and so did I. Gnr Tuck had to be carried to bed, goodness knows who was sober enough to carry him. I lost my teeth and found them in the grass the next morning.

There was very little to do as we were waiting to be dispersed in the afternoon. It was well, that there was little to do because most of us were not fit to get up. We paid for it alright and it cured us of drinking Calvados, it also made us very careful with Cognac. I do not think that any of us have tasted Calvados since then, I certainly haven't. The very smell of it makes my stomach heave. We have had ample opportunity to drink it, but we leave it alone. Since then we heard of a chap in the 25pdr unit who had too much of it and died during the night; tough luck.

I had to go to Cahagnes to draw water and it took me twice as long as usual.

During the afternoon, they began to sort us out and check all the handing over of equipment. Guns and lorries etc. L troop were to take over A Trp's SP guns, they had had trailer guns up to this time. We had tea and were all set as the new L Troop to move off at about 6 o'clock p.m. The rest of the troop was still waiting to be dispersed to infantry. We said all our goodbyes and moved off at 6'30 up to St Mesnil Azouf, close to our BHQ. We were to spend the next three days of 'rest' in getting the men used to the new guns; that meant a lot of gun drill. They put a load of work in that first day and then late in the evening the order came round *"prepare to move"*. This was the second time that this had happened and we began to wonder if there was only one Div (the 43rd) in the 2nd Army as they could not afford to let us rest.

This was about the time that the American's were breaking out and beginning to form what later became known as the Falaise 'pocket'.

Our Div had to go in again to help press the attack and that was that; it meant that the guns were to move forward the following morning. They did so. I went up with water later in the day and found THQ at Re Plessis Grimault; this was a village just beyond Mont Pincon.

Our route lay up Mont Pincon along the crest of the hill for about four miles then through the village. The weather was hotter than ever; the dust was terrific. The flies were still more numerous, but worse than ever was the terrible stink. I thought that it was impossible to have any worse stink than around Cheux but this beat Cheux.

Down in one hollow there was about five dead horses on the road, the tanks had gone over them and flattened them out, no one had time to move the remains so all the traffic just kept going over what were now just several heaps of mess. Imagine that under several days of sunshine. There were still dead bodies of men lying at the side of the road over Mont Pincon and in one place three of our Sherman Tanks had been burnt out.

As we approached the village there was a lovely Tiger with his teeth drawn, right on the crossroads. They were massive monsters and wicked looking b------s. We went through the village, it had been badly hit, and went along a track to find THQ. We stopped to ask about it and there was some infantry digging in at the roadside. Immediately they began to shout, *"Shift that bloody truck"*. We asked *"Why?"* and they said *"He shells us every time a truck stops here"*. We got going.

We found THQ about half a mile further in and they had already had a doze. They were in a deserted farmhouse and were doing the cooking in a thick walled outhouse. No casualties though except for minor injuries so that was OK. I went round sites; they were OK, a bit of shellfire but nothing really close.

There were a few bodies lying around with blankets over them to keep the flies off. Some of the dead beasts were so covered with flies that you could hardly see any part of the beast itself.

I went back to St Mesnil. We were not in Brigade A Ech now but all the soft vehicles had been left behind thus forming an A Ech of our own.

Above: The British Projector Infantry Anti-Tank (PIAT). First used during the invasion of Sicily in 1943, the PIAT had an effective range of 350 yards (320m) but did have the advantage of no smoke discharge from the muzzle that other systems displayed, giving away the firers position.

Below: The German Ferdinand Tank. Designed by Porsche, the Ferdinand (later the *Elefant*) was the first of a new breed of German *Jagdpanzers* (tank-hunters) with enclosed crew compartment and greatly improved armour. These 65 ton hunting tanks sought to seek and destroy allied armour, with their twin air cooled engines and 88mm guns.

Above: Arthur and friends at an improvised 'barber's shop', somewhere in northwest Europe. He is carrying a 9mm Sten Gun, a short-barrelled automatic weapon issued to those fighting at close range, such as commandos and those who may need a rapid and heavy weight of fire during self-defence. Its short barrel and folding stock also meant that it could be brought into action quickly, from the cramped confines of a vehicle.

Below: Another giant of the battlefield, a Sherman tank at the D-Day Museum, Portsmouth; a relative lightweight (30 tons) but with far superior armour than its German counterparts.

CHAPTER SEVEN
GOOD GERMANS

Same again
2/11/44

Dear Oll,

I went up again to Troop and sites the next day, they were still around Le Plessis Grimault and then we got orders to move our A Ech vehicles forward. This was about the 12th Aug and we set out, up Mont Pincon to Le Plessis Grimbault, then turned sharp left towards Aunay-Sur-Odon. This took us right over the summit of Mont Pincon; there was a fine view of the surrounding country from here. We did not loiter too long as we were too conspicuous up there in the bright sunshine. We went downhill towards Aunay and pulled in to a field just before we reached Roucamps.

We were definitely moving forward nowadays at a fair rate. On July 29th we were at Livry in front of Caumont; now we were here, sited around Le Plessis Grimbault, which meant we had advanced quite a fair distance.

There was a lot of evidence too that Jerry was beginning to move in a hurry: there were his tanks and guns scattered over wide areas; in Caumont there was an 88 field gun and a half-track vehicle jammed in a gateway as if they had both tried to get out in a hurry. Near Roucamps an 88 was left in perfect condition along with ammo. Also at Le Plessis a 105mm Howitzer in good condition with ammo. There was an SP gun that must be at least six-inch calibre but that had been knocked out like the Tiger.

We dug in at Roucamps although I do not think that we need to have done so; still better to be sure than sorry.

Took water up again the next day; THQ and sites were still in same places. They were getting an occasional 'cruncher' but nothing serious.

I had been getting water from a little stream near Furgues but that was a long way back now. So, after looking on the map I decided to go to Aunay-Sur-Odon as there was a river there. I went through Roucamps and over a range of thickly wooded hills that gave a view for miles; we could see Aunay down on the plain as we came over the hills. What a surprise we got when we approached the place. The fields on either side were just a mass of bomb craters, big bombs too. The town itself was even worse; this place had just been smashed up. I thought that I had seen some places that were knocked about but this was different to anything that I had seen before. Our aircraft had raided this place. What an awful sight, there was not a building left except the church tower, everything was reduced to rubble and the roads were just paths between piles of rubbish. God knows how many people were still underneath that lot; there must be some. Everything had been blasted to hell; even the orchards on the edge of town had been blasted. Every tree had either been uprooted or shattered. You just simply cannot imagine what the destruction was like.

The river was still running though; neither bombs nor shells can stop rivers or streams. I filled up alright and went back still thinking of Aunay.

The next day Troop moved and I took water up to them. They were now in a farm along with the guns; it was as usual, deserted and there was Jerry equipment about the place showing that they had been in occupation before us. I did not go back that day, the other A Ech vehicles were brought up instead. We were now concentrated again.

It had been a fairly prosperous farm and there was still some livestock about including chickens. There was a full barrel of Calvados too; that didn't interest myself and several others, it was too recent after the last do. Some of the other chaps started fetching it out in bottles; it was not too long before they were tottering, and of course we could afford to laugh at them, to think what they would feel like in the morning. We were waiting for orders and it was pretty easy for us while we waited.

There was a good well here, but it went dry when I started drawing too much water from it. I had to go back to Duval for it now, this was about 8 miles back.

We invented a new game here, we all started making rounds of the chicken nests for eggs. We got quite a few but it developed to such a pitch that the poor old hens didn't know what to do. No sooner did a hen go into a nest than there was a soldier at hand, waiting for the egg. The poor old hens didn't know whether to sit tight or take flight. They were good eggs though and before our chaps left here several of the chickens had finished their laying career; they were fairly tough.

On about the 20th THQ and the guns moved forward again about four miles, through Courville and sighted around Brigade HQ. I took water up and found them alright. It was a bit nasty getting to No 4 Gun owing to minefields, they were in a cornfield and there was white tape everywhere; that signifies mines and that they have not yet been cleared. On one track there was a Cromwell Tank and a Bren Carrier that had got their lot with Teller mines. I found the gun's tracks and kept dead in the same tracks.

The next day while I was at THQ (it was in a field), we heard a slight shrill, it was a lovely sunny day and we had seen aircraft flying about, they were Thunderbolts so we took no notice. A few minutes later we heard a machine gun fire and looked up; it was only a couple of those Thunderbolts and we didn't know what to make of it. They came diving down again, guns blazing and we did not know whether to get in a trench or what. Up they went and down again; we got in trenches, this was serious. They played around for about ten minutes and then cleared off. We got up and made inquiries; they had shot up a carrier on the crossroads about 100yds up the road, so we came to the conclusion that it must have been two of our planes that Jerry had captured and was now using against us. Actually it turned out to be a mistake by the two pilots, they should have been attacking the next crossroads.

Troop moved again now to Proussy in a farmhouse again. I was now fetching water from Duval and taking it up beyond Proussy which was a journey of about 23 miles. We now moved up to just beyond Courville into a big orchard; it was dark when we arrived and fortunately there was plenty of trenches about, ready dug. We got down to sleep in them but it started to pour down with rain and those who had not troubled to cover their trenches soon got flooded. They sheltered under the trucks.

Jerry was at this time well in the 'Falaise Pocket' and the gap was beginning to narrow. Our really big guns had moved up to the same locality as we were in, the front was still moving forward.

I went up to Troop again and the chaps had found a barrel of Cognac. Now that was decent stuff and I had a drop in a cup of tea. I also took a bottle back with me; I was very careful with it though.

Outside the orchard there was three Jerry half-track vehicles all smashed up and turned over into the ditch. Our Typhoons had been busy.

During the second day here we saw some new troops moving up. All their brass was polished and their webbing Blancoed[28]. We laughed at that, it was evident that they had only just come from the beaches. A few days in the line would soon take the shine off their brass.

We heard the best news that we had heard for a long time this day. We were told that our artillery could not find a target and that our patrols could not contact Jerry. This meant that he was on the run. He was on the run alright. The third day, Troop moved again and an officer took me up in the evening; we did about 20 miles I think. We were advancing alright, we arrived at St Honorine La Chardonne, about 15 miles from Falaise and our infantry had just cleared the village.

We expected to stay here for several days but we now came under CRA instead of Brigade and we moved again the next day. I was now staying with THQ and we all moved through Athis to Le Pont, a little village halfway between Flers and Conde Sur Noireau. We were to give ack-ack protection to two bridges across a river.

We stayed here for almost a week and it was nice and quiet; it was almost rest to us. We stayed in a farm and slept in a barn. It was a treat.

We had only been here two days when we got news that our Colonel had had it. It was true, he was dead right enough. Apparently he was

---

[28] A cleaning compound historically used by the British Army to whiten leather equipment.

travelling in the neighbourhood of Conde in his Jeep, when he had to stop because the road was blocked with traffic; he wanted to push on and told the driver to go round and on the grass verge. That was his lot; a mine put paid to that Jeep. The driver got off with serious wounds but the old man had finished his journey. That did not affect us much, as men who do silly things like that are easy to replace.

We had a nice easy time here and it was a lovely place. It is generally called Normandy's little Switzerland. The river winds along a long valley for about twelve miles between steep hills and was a pleasure to ride along it. It was just like the pictures that Nestle used to have on their adverts.

I had occasion to go through Conde and that was another mess. Our aircraft had raided the place and they had left it the same as Aunay but on a bigger scale. These were the two worst places that I had yet seen, worse than Caen. The 'Falaise Pocket' was getting very small and tight now and Jerry was breaking up.

About the 29th we moved; we were on the north side of the pocket and moved south, right through what had been the pocket a few days before. Down on the south side we deployed our guns around our Div concentration area, about half way between Tromental and Ecouche. We were about ten miles from Argentan.

During the journey we had seen a hell of a lot of Jerry's smashed equipment, and good Germans, dead ones. We stayed here for three days and had time to look around; there was Jerry equipment everywhere. There was a big move coming off but we did not know what it was yet. We got to know soon enough.

Our Div had been given the task of putting a bridge across the Seine. The Americans were across at Sens, south of Paris and they were up to the river, but not across it all the way from Paris to Vernon. The river was a good width at Vernon but that was the place chosen, because of roads I think. Plans were made and the job was done but it was no easy task.

We were 100 miles from Vernon and had to time our movements to work with the Americans. You just cannot block the roads with convoys at your leisure. It turned out that we could not get all the Div through, so we just had to do it with one brigade (ours), plus all the Div's artillery and six tanks. The place was recced very thoroughly and the position was that Vernon was held by about 300 Americans; Vernonnet, on the other side of the river was held by the Germans. The other side was overlooked by steep hills which came down to ground level about 300 yards away from the river. The hills on our side (Vernon) sloped more gently down to the town and then the river. There was two blown up bridges and two islands in the middle, one above and one below the bridge. Jerry had got positions on the hills and in trenches at the river edge.

The Americans and the Germans were taking things easy and not bothering each other much at all. Our officers examined the whole layout without letting themselves be seen and got information from the Free-French[29] in regard to the depth of the water. They were told that the water above the south island was deep enough to sail Ducks through and that the water on the other side of the north island was shallow enough to walk through. The whole secret of this plan was to keep Jerry ignorant of our plans of making a bridge and not let him know that there was any British troops nearer than 400 miles.

We set off for Vernon on the morning of the 23rd of Aug; we arrived at Vernon in the early afternoon of the 24th. Our infantry was disposed all around the back streets of the town that were near the river. There was Ducks and Bren Carriers, the six tanks and a lot of bridge building material. These were all got into the town and hidden away without being seen from the other side of the river. At 6'30p.m. our guns opened up on the German positions; a fairly heavy barrage. At ten minutes to seven our infantry then began to move across the river in Ducks. It was now getting dark but there was a lot of fire coming from the other side. We were sending a lot of smoke shells across too. All the next day we kept on shelling, both explosive and smoke.

The infantry got across without losses and the REs started to build a pontoon bridge. The tanks were ferried across and did good work. The infantry began to push inland despite the good positions that Jerry had on the hills. We could see our own artillery shells actually exploding.

They made a complete pontoon bridge and our Bren Carriers and all that sort of stuff began to stream across. By this time our infantry had reached a village, La Chapelle St Ouen about three miles away and were fighting like hell.

As Jerry fell back he began to shell us; he did so, so heavily that the REs had to withdraw off the river for some time. At one point Jerry broke the bridge with a shell and it had to have another section put in.

A lot of stuff, our brigade stuff, including our own unit went over to the other side, over what was really a flimsy bridge. As we drove across, it rose and fell like waves.

It was now the morning of the 26th and our guns were deployed around the bridge on the Vernonnet side; we drove into a sports ground about 100yds from our bridge and started to establish THQ. We were looking inside some wooden huts (dressing rooms), wondering if they would do to sleep in, when the old familiar whistle came and we went down. We had no trenches as we had only just got in, so we got as flat as

---

[29] A French movement organized in London by Charles de Gaulle to fight for the liberation of France from German control and for the restoration of the republic.

possible on the floor. It was a full salvo, about eight shells and it shook us. One hit a house about 20yds away and wrecked it completely. One dropped about 30yds over us and hit some Tank Corps chaps, killed one and wounded five others pretty badly. We got up, no casualties among us, and began to look for cover. Immediately another salvo came over. Believe me they are terrifying when they come close; I saw several of these burst across the playing pitch but they were not so close to us as the last salvo was.

He hit the bridge with this salvo and broke it again. One of our DRs was waiting to go across, he dived into a hole and when he got up and saw the broken bridge he thanked his lucky star that he was not on it when that shell dropped. It only took two hours to put right again.

We started to dig trenches again, as fast as we could. There was no more shelling after that for the whole time that we were there (six days). We found the groundsman's place, it was half below ground level and we decided to sleep there.

The next day the REs began to put a Bailey bridge[30] across and then another one; this made it possible to have one way traffic across both Bailey bridges and all back traffic had to use the small pontoon bridge.

Well this was our job done and all we had to do now was to defend the bridgehead. Our heavy stuff began to stream over, tanks, guns and everything else. For four solid days and nights this stuff kept on coming without a break; there was never a moment without a stream of traffic on the bridges. I think the whole second army came over. This was the start of the famous drive through Amiens to Brussels and Antwerp.

We were glad to see all this stuff and felt rather proud of ourselves; we felt that we had done a good job of work. We were all given a day off in turn and I went across the river to Vernon, I bought the postcards that I sent you that day and a loaf of French bread - we had been on biscuits for ten days.

After we had been over several days and things got quiet, the REs began getting the casualties out of the river. These casualties were the cost of that great dash to Belgium and those poor b------s did not get any cheers or praise, just a white cross and some flowers. They lie along the riverbank.

If Jerry had known that we were going to try and bridge the river at that point, I think that he would have stopped us because from those hills, he could have taken full command of that part of the river. He did not know and that was the secret to our success.

We now moved about six miles along the river to St Genevieve (village) and had a well-earned rest. We stayed here for 11 days.

---

[30] A temporary bridge formed or prefabricated from interchangeable steel truss panels, bolted together. Named after its British designer, Sir Donald Bailey.

THE INFANTRY NEVER WAVERED!

SOMERSET MEN'S GRIM STRUGGLE

SPLENDID VICTORY ON MONT PINCON

CORPS COMMANDER PRAISES THEIR VALOUR

BY A MILITARY OBSERVER

A glorious page in the war history of the 43rd (Wessex) Division was the assault on the 1,200-foot Mont Pincon, highest point in Normandy's "Little Switzerland," which was triumphantly stormed by troops of this Division.

It is a story of West country infantrymen, including battalions of the Somersets and Wiltshires, pinned to the ground for six and seven hours ham. "I tried to get a section round the right flank, but they were also pinned down. We couldn't see the Germans but knew near enough from where they were firing. On the spur of the moment, I picked up a German machine gun which we had captured, went up on to the bank, and fired on the German machine guns in the farm. They stopped firing and I got back under cover."

Above: Dated 23rd September 1944, one of Arthur's cuttings celebrates the hard won victory on Mont Pincon. Another cutting **below** is entitled 'Troops embarking in assault boats to make the first crossing of the Seine at Vernon on the evening of 25th August 1944.'

Left: The British four-engine Lancaster bomber. Participated in 156'000 sorties, it was the main bomber used in the strategic bombing offensive over Europe. It carried bombs up to 12'000lb and was famously modified to accept the 'Dambusters' bouncing-bomb.

Below: *'...they made a complete pontoon bridge and our Bren Carriers and all that sort of stuff began to stream across.'*

CHAPTER EIGHT
INTO BELGIUM

Same again

Dear Oll,

Just arrived at St Genevieve and we did not know yet that we were to rest here, we actually deployed our guns for the first two days. We were feeling rather proud of ourselves about this time because we (129 Brigade) were the first British troops to cross the River Seine and we felt that we were entitled to a decent rest. It was here that we first saw several French women who had, had their heads shaved. We thought this was rotten and silly, these women were supposed to be collaborators and may have deserved punishment but we thought that the people who were so brave as to shave women's heads had not been so brave when Jerry was there; they only found their courage after we arrived. We thought that it would have been better for them to have got a Sten and gone for Jerry.

It was here that we had grapes straight from the vineyard and peaches from the trees. There was what we considered to be a joke going on here too, the villagers here understood us to be the SS troops of the British Army. This made us laugh and we asked them who had told them this and they said *"The Germans"*. This made us laugh more so.

We were billeted in a decent big house and were very comfortable. We had the wireless and the weather was good, so it was OK. I went to an ENSA[31] show in Vernon and it was pretty good.

While Phil and I were drawing water one day at a little stream between St Genevieve and Gommecourt a lady from Gommecourt came to the stream to do her washing, after some conversation with Phil, she invited us to go to her house for tea on the Sunday. These people hereabouts looked on us as their liberators and they treated us very well indeed. We had a really good meal as I wrote and told you, and on the day that we left the district, she piled us up with apples, pears & peaches etc. We had quite a few eggs and other things given to us from other people in the village.

One day we had a run up the hills behind Gamecourt and from the top, looking east, we had a fine view. The hills on our side all sloped down

---

[31] The Entertainments National Service Association was an organisation set up in 1939 to provide entertainment for British armed forces personnel during World War II. ENSA operated as part of the Navy, Army and Air Force Institutes (NAAFI).

very sharply to the river Seine, which wound round in the sweeping curves here. On the far side, the country rolled away into the distance comparatively. We could see many miles and a good stretch of the river below us. On our side of the river we could see several villages nestling on the hillside including La Rochelle.

At this village there was a tremendous big chateau and this had been used for an HQ by Jerry. It was to this chateau that Field Marshall Rommel was brought after he was wounded. He died here. He was a good German.[32]

We were listening one night to the news and the war report on the wireless when we got a surprise, it was some big general talking and he started to talk about Mont Pincon and the crossing of the River Seine. Well we all remembered these two jobs, only too well and we knew what he was talking about. His remarks pleased us though; he said *"Mont Pincon was the place where the 'guts' was torn out of the German Army"* and that the way in which we had crossed the Seine was a classic. This was true.

After we had been here several days, someone discovered a brothel in Vernon; quite a good few of the chaps went to it 100 francs a time, and we all had a lot of laughs out of it. One night, six of them went down and there was only one woman working there at the time, but she polished them off in an hour! We laughed like hell when they described it to us afterwards; how they queued up to wait for each other, how they stood there with nothing on while she washed it for them. Cold water too; that fetched a laugh. How they had it washed again afterwards and then how they had to hurry and dress and make room for the next one. We even laugh nowadays about it. One of the chaps said it was just like buying a pound of sausage.

We had quite a decent time and rest here; the weather was good and we didn't do too much work. There was no noise of gunfire and the whole place had assumed a peaceful aspect. We began to wonder whether or not we had been overlooked and forgotten. We hoped so.

After 10 days we had orders to prepare to move and we moved on the 11th. It was now the 14th Sept and we moved off about dinnertime. We were to harbour for the night about five miles beyond Mons in Belgium. It was well over a hundred miles away and a late start like that meant that we should be driving through the night. We did not like that. On the top of that we only progressed very slowly. It was a Div move and that meant a

---

[32] Unbeknown to Arthur, Rommel had actually taken his own life after being linked to the conspiracy to assassinate Adolf Hitler. Because Rommel was a national hero, Hitler desired to eliminate him quietly and therefore forced his suicide by cyanide pill, in return for assurance that Rommel's family would not be persecuted after his death.

very long column. We carried on through Cheauvais[33] towards Amiens. We passed to the east of Amiens and crossed the River Somme. We came through Breteuil and as we approached the river Somme we could see the twin towers of Amiens Cathedral, away on our left.

Through the Somme battlefield to Moreuil, then Albert, to Bapaume and on to Cambrai. We had several reminders of the last war as we passed graveyards which were the fruits of the fighting that took place hereabouts. All the names of these places were familiar to me as ancient battlefields and I could well imagine in this type of country the trench warfare that was endured in '14 to '18. Flat rolling country with vast bare spaces and few natural born trees, all tending to encourage trench warfare with its consequent mud & slush and frostbitten feet etc.

The roads are long straight stretches of avenue, miles and miles of straightness and tall trees planted along each side until it becomes monotonous in itself; and yet if they did not plant any trees, the countryside would be very monotonous.

Somewhere about here we passed a monument to the Tank Regiments. It was erected on the spot where tanks were first brought into action against the enemy, this blasted same enemy.

We also saw a miniature submarine left on the side of the road by Jerry in his hurry to get back, goodness knows how a thing like that got here, it had a torpedo tube on either side of it.

As we passed through Bapaume and went towards Cambrai it was getting late and dark so we thought that a breakdown would be useful now. There was nearly another 60 miles to do and we knew that with a big column like this that it would take most of the night to do it. When about 4 four or five miles short of Cambrai, sure enough we got a breakdown; our engine became overheated so we stopped and fell out of the convoy.

We had been greeted with cheers, smiles and hand waving all the way so far and we were trusting that the people here would be friendly. We found a café; it was closed but we could see a light in an inner room so we gave a knock. A man answered and we asked if we could put the truck in the yard for the night. Apparently the yard belonged to the chap next door so he got him out and he said it was OK. Then he showed us a barn with electric light and plenty of good clean straw; what more could we ask?

We got the truck in and got some rations off, tinned meat and veg, took them into the café and he invited us into his kitchen while he heated them up. We had a good supper and he gave us a couple of glasses of beer each; not as good as our beer back home but it was OK at a time like that.

---

[33] Arthur had highlighted this place name, perhaps for future review as the editor has been unable to locate it. It is likely however to be Beauvais, near Amiens.

We pulled in here at half nine and got down to kip before eleven; our people did not get in at their destinations until 5a.m. next morning. We got up at six o'clock and washed and shaved, then we were going to make tea when the people here invited us into their house for a cup of coffee. Of course that was OK with us. We packed our blankets etc., had the coffee, gave the lady a tablet of soap and set off again about 7'15a.m.

On through Cambrai to Valenciennes (famous for its lace). About 12 kilometres short of this place we found one of our guns and detachment at the side of the road. They had got a puncture in their trailer wheel; they were just having breakfast, so we had a cup of tea.

We carried on over the Belgium frontier and here in the villages they had all got their flags out; everybody was only too ready to wave to us. This southern part of Belgium is a coal mining area and the sight of big dirt heaps and colliery pithead gear reminded me of home. We stopped to pick up a shovel that had fell off a Bren Carrier and a chap on the roadside spoke to us in good English, he said that we should find plenty of friends here in Belgium.

We were now travelling on our own and making pretty good time as we reached Mons. The people were eager to help us whenever we were doubtful of the way. It was now about 8'50a.m.

Passed the [railway] station and for the first time since leaving England I saw a railway engine; it had steam up too, but no train. Then we saw what I take to be their tram service. It is three or four trams or carriages linked together and they run on a railway track at the side of the road. No fence between the road and the rail track and it did seem queer to me to see what was almost like a train running along the street.

We had to make a detour because there was a bridge blown up but we found our troop and arrived at 9'15a.m. and had some breakfast. This meant that we had done a journey in two hours of daylight that it took our convoys seven hours to do in the darkness; we had had a good seven hours sleep, the rest of the troop had only had two.

We set out again in the convoy at about 12'30 and headed for Saignes (*swah-nee*) then Brame Le court and on to Waterloo, which is south-east of Brussels. We saw the monument here that was put up to commemorate the battle of Waterloo, it is a figure of a lion placed on the summit of a high mound. Then to Louvain; there is some lovely buildings here. On to Diest and about three kilometres short of the Albert canal. We arrived here at 2'30a.m. got down to kip in a barn; up at 4a.m., on guard till 5a.m. then slept till 8a.m. The ration truck had got lost so we only had a scratch breakfast; it came in at 10'30a.m.

We had been feted all the way up from France; every place in Belgium turned out in strength to wave and cheer, to ask for souvenirs or cigs. They were chucking fruit to us all the way: apples, pears, tomatoes, etc. We had a good load by the time that we arrived in.

It did us good to see these happy people, they were happy because we, as the British Army were here and Jerry was running away.

    So long & love
    Yours,
        Arth.

    XXXXXXX

Above: Although the German *Kriegsmarine* produced a number of mini submarines, Arthur almost certainly saw the two-man *Seehund* (Seal). It saw operational service from January 1945 onwards.

Below: From Arthur's cuttings: *'Infantry with Bren Carriers wait by the roadside before moving up for the attack on Mont Pincon.'* The highest point in the region and therefore of strategic importance during the Battle of Normandy, Mont Pincon was the objective of Operation Bluecoat during July and August of 1944.

CHAPTER NINE
TAKE ALL RISKS

Same again
22/11/44

Dear Oll,

At last I find myself with a few minutes to spare and am able to continue.

We had arrived at Lummev in Belgium at nearly 3a.m. on Sat 16/9/44, we had to do guard in turns and we were up at 8 o'clock for breakfast. It was hardly a breakfast as we usually know it.

You see the ration truck failed to arrive with us so our captain set out in his Jeep at 3a.m. to try and find it, that was an almost impossible task but I gave him full marks for turning out and making an effort at that hour in the morning, and pitch dark too.

He returned at 5a.m. without the truck, but he had raised some odd rations from somewhere, tinned sausages and a few biscuits; that was breakfast and we had to manage.

The truck and cooks turned up at about 10'30 so we were OK for dinner. My problem was water and there was quite a big stream which drove a mill wheel in this farm; it looked pretty horrible water and I decided that I would not attempt to use it except as an absolute last resort. I went on a recce. I understood there to be an authorised water point at Beeringen, but I could not get there because the roads were so full of convoy traffic.

I could not find any other suitable water so I went farther upstream, about two miles up the same stream that runs through the farm, it was much clearer up there and I drew a couple of hundred gallons.

I pulled up at the stream and got our apparatus working nicely when along comes a boy about eight years with a couple of eggs for us, very nice that. The nearest houses were about 100 yards away and apparently these people had seen us and sent the eggs across so we gave the kiddy a bar of chocolate.

It takes about three quarters of an hour to pump a tank of water and we had time to spare while the pump was working, so we tried to talk to the boy. It was difficult as French was useless here. Anyway, in less than ten minutes we had a crowd of about 15 people around and we were learning to count in Flemish, (they say *Flamsh*) *"eine, tween, tri, etc"*.

We spent the rest of the day attending to our engines etc. to keep them up to scratch.

We were sleeping on the top of a barn full of straw, about 20 feet up just under the roof, but it was comfortable. It was a bit of a nuisance though climbing down a vertical ladder in blackness just to relieve ourselves.

The next day, Sunday, I went farther up for water and drew it from out of the Albert Canal. I suppose that you have heard of it. We had bridges across (pontoon) and I had to get my water from the other side as I could not get low enough to the water on our side.

I was very much surprised at the size of this canal. It was some obstacle, speaking in regard to war. It was good quality water though.

This Sunday afternoon we were told of our next objective: we were told the story of how paratroops were to be dropped at Maastright, Eindhoven, Grave, Nijmegen and Arnheim and how we (our 30 Corps) and two other corps were to drive a corridor right up through Holland and connecting all the places together. Our ultimate objective was much farther on but I cannot tell of that yet a while.

We were to drive on as the centre of the corridor, the other corps to keep pace with us and protect our flanks. The newspapers must have told you how long and slender that corridor was, we did not need to be told.

Anyway, we left Lummev on Monday 19/9/44 and bivouacked in some woods near Bourg Leopold. The paratroops had by now been dropped at several appointed places and were doing some hard fighting.

I fetched water from Bourg Leopold, this was a peacetime garrison town and there was a huge barracks covering a big area just on the edge of town. There were signs (plenty) of air raid destruction here and a civilian told us that our planes had raided the barracks and killed 5000 Germans, nice work eh?

We left this place at 6a.m. on the 21/9/44 and made our way over the Dutch border. By this time the way was fairly clear up as far as Grave, as there had not been a great amount of opposition up to here. Despite this fact we did not get on too fast; we had to stand for several hours at one place to let a bridging convoy go through.

We passed through Aalst and saw a bunch of about 30 collaborators that the Free-Dutch had just rounded up.

We went through Eindhoven just as it was going dark and made our way to Grave. We went over the Maas bridge here at Grave at 3'15a.m. 22/9/44. It is a very long bridge and our airborne troops had done a good job of work by taking this bridge intact.

We pulled into a farmyard at 3'30a.m. and got ready to get some sleep. We had been on the road for 2½ hours driving through the night and we needed sleep badly. Imagine what we felt like when we were told that reveille was to be at 5'30a.m. They finished up by making reveille at 7a.m. and we got about three hours sleep, had breakfast and then took to the road again.

It seemed that the Yank Airborne had had difficulty in clearing Nijmegen of the enemy so we had to send some tanks and infantry into the bridge area.

We pulled into the town and parked, there was nothing that we could do until the bridge question had been settled either for us or against us. The people here were overjoyed and brought us apples and pears etc.

We slept in a builder's shed that night and no one strayed very far away after dark; there was quite a lot of spasmodic shooting going on by collaborators and Germans that had been left behind, everyone walked around with his finger on his trigger.

On the way up we saw nine of our Sherman Tanks that had been ambushed and knocked out by a couple of Jerry's 88 millimetre guns. Jerry had hidden these two guns very well and our tanks had been pushing on at a good rate. The German gunners waited for the tanks to pass and then let go; they put paid to nine of them before other tanks could get to work on their 88s. Of course they got their 'lot' but they had done a good days work from their point of view.

I spoke to one chap that was a survivor from one of the tanks and he said it was bloody horrible. Their tank did not set on fire and they managed to get out. All they could do then was take cover and listen to the horrible screams of men in the other tanks that did get alight. There was nothing they could do to release them as the turret covers are locked from the inside.

We moved to another part of the town (Nijmegen) next day to a garage that Jerry had been using. There was billets over the garage and Jerry had gone in a hurry, leaving a lot of junk behind. It was here that I found that airman's forage cap, the ring and a fountain pen that will be OK when I can make a small cork washer for it.

We were allowed to walk out in the evening but not singly, must be at least two together; that was OK in a place like this with shots cracking out at odd intervals.

Two of us, Fred Webber and myself found a baker's shop and got a couple of loaves for some cigs. We saw the flash of a rifle that fired several rounds about a 100yds away from us. We tried to contact that shooter. We must have lost him in the dark because when we got close enough to challenge the man who we thought had fired, we found that we were holding up an American. Naturally, he was a bit scared when we poked a loaded Sten Gun into him. We could not trust anyone in the dark so we searched him; we did not find any arms on him so we passed him on, to his great relief.

By this time the bridge was definitely in our hands and our Div was moving on towards Elst which is about 4½ miles short of Arnheim[34].

The paratroops at Arnheim had been having a bad time for about eight days and they were in a bad way. We had watched a lot of supplies being flown on to these chaps by fleets of Dakota aircraft, but the plans of getting up to Arnheim to relieve them had not worked according to plan. The Corp that were supposed to move up as protection for our flanks had failed to keep up the pace and now there was only the 30th Corps, (43rd and 50th Infantry Divs plus One Armoured Div) who were faced with the job of fighting their way from Nijmegen to Arnheim: 12 miles of flat country with the River Lek immediately in front of Arnheim.

There was a row of hills just behind Arnheim which provided Jerry with excellent observation and gun positions.

Beside all this we had to provide our own flank protection and the enemy was in some good strength. Nevertheless, something had to be done to reach the airborne troops and our Corps received the order to *"take all risks"*. That speaks for itself of what sort of job it was to be. It proved to be a hellish business.

Our Div deployed to attack Elst, with the aid of tanks, the 50th deployed to protect our flank as the enemy was strong on that side; there was little opposition on the left.

After some sharp fighting and heavy artillery fire we took the village and moved in, in force, our brigade was now detailed to protect the left flank as our other brigade fought their way to the River Lek. We could plainly see Arnheim and the airborne troops were getting desperate.

Other things happened now that made the job in hand more difficult than ever. Tanks could not deploy because of soft ground, they had to be recalled and the infantry were left to do the job with artillery support. Another factor was that Jerry cut our corridor between Eindhoven and Grave and that left us cut off for a short while. This interfered with our supplies of rations and ammunition. Fortunately we had captured a Jerry ration dump and they issued these; they were not good but they helped us over a bad spot. There was also cigars (good ones), spirits, rum, gin etc. This was issued and helped a lot.

214 Brigade got up to the river and also got about 800 men across (Dorset Regt) but it was impossible to get across in strength with any heavy stuff. The order now was that under the circumstances the Airborne were to be withdrawn under our Div protection. I think that it was Tuesday night 26/9/44 (or Mon 25th)[35] when they were evacuated across the river. About

---

[34] Curiously, Arthur uses the German name for Arnhem, perhaps hinting at the source of his maps.

[35] The withdrawal took place on the 25th Sept 1944; an ignominious end to

2000 paratroops and most of our infantry were withdrawn.

We gave all the artillery support possible and there was one of our troops (Bofors Guns) that moved right up to the river bank in the dark, deployed and proceeded to bash away for most of the night, just to keep Jerry occupied while our air troops got back over the river. They moved back before daylight and Jerry started to press strongly over the bridge. Our chaps held on for some time but had to give way under very heavy pressure.

The battle developed and a pretty rough time ensued for our Div. We had a THQ on the west side of the village of Elst and Jerry slammed shells into that village continuously for the whole of the time that we were there (ten days). We got quite used to the sound of bursting shells and unless they were really close to us we did not take cover.

We knew that our people thought that there was a chance of us giving ground because there was several Tiger Tanks lying about the place that our infantry had knocked out and the REs now came round, put charges in the gun barrels and blew the ends off. This was done so that Jerry could not use them again if he did recapture them.

The infantry kept bringing in batches of prisoners and one of these batches was attacked by one Typhoon with rockets because he thought that they were the enemy infiltrating through our lines. Poor buggers. Rockets are nice to watch from a distance.

On Sunday 1st Oct about ten of us were to go to the mobile baths about three miles towards Nijmegen. We had to go through the village (Elst) and there was a road junction that was usually getting shelled; Jerry was making it a target in the hope of hitting traffic.

When anyone had to take a truck through the village, they used to make a good speed and get round this corner as quick as possible. We were swinging round this corner at a fair belt when someone stopped us to tow their truck out of the ditch. It was quiet at the moment but we did not like it as we knew that there would soon be some shells. We got out and sure enough we had to dive in the ditch; about seven or eight 88s started cracking, we then got up and made our way to an empty house about 40yds down the road. We just about made it when a dozen came over. We all got down the cellar and had a smoke and a laugh; we can always laugh afterwards if there are no casualties.

The Bridge at Nijmegen was a very big and solid affair, it needed to be so, as it was our lifeline and Jerry was continually attacking it with aircraft.

Operation Market Garden, now widely known through the 1977 epic war film A Bridge Too Far. The Allies suffered as many as 17'000 casualties during this operation, of which some 1'500 were from Arthur's XXX Corps. The Germans did not get off lightly, with as many as 8'000 casualties.

We needed it now more so than ever, as the enemy was attacking very strongly and we were using a lot of heavy artillery ammunition. It did get hit by bombs but very little damage was done and it did not stop traffic. It did get broken though in a very surprising manner that I cannot tell you about yet[36]. It took the REs 24 hours to build a short bridge over the gap in the original bridge and so reopen it to traffic.

This had serious repercussions as far as we were concerned, it was already a difficult job to get enough supplies of ammo and rations up and this buggered us up some more. Artillery ammo had to be rationed and this meant that we could not give the support to the already hard-pressed infantry that we should have done.

It was a rough time and the infantry fought dammed well to hold the enemy despite the fact that they had to give some ground. He was very active with patrols too; one patrol about 30 strong got through at night from the east to the road (our only route). Fortunately they were seen in time and destroyed. We could not stand the supply route being cut any more.

Our billet was about 300yds as the crow flies from the church in the centre of the village and the tower was being used by our people as an OP. It was hit by German shell fire many times but it was strongly built and survived until the afternoon Jerry managed to set the church on fire. It burnt slowly from about 4p.m. until 7p.m. when it got a real hold and flames began to leap in the air. It was dark now and the tower also was well alight. We all stood and watched this terrific beacon as it blazed up in the darkness. It was a real sight to watch it blazing; about 8'30p.m. the top caved in amid a shower of sparks and the whole countryside was now lit up.

It is now the 1/1/45 and at last I get down to write a bit more of this story: We were needless to say always on the alert for 'stray' shells, and there was almost a continuous rattle of machine gun fire. This was now 'usual' and we did not worry much about it. First a Bren would open up, and then a Spandau[37] and they both rattle death.

We had a laugh when listening to the news on two days. We had been in the village of Elst for about four days and it was quiet except for shelling;

---

[36] It is not clear what incident Arthur refers to here, but it is known that the bridge was subjected to repeated German attacks in order to prevent XXX Corps pushing on to Arnhem. As well as being shelled, the Germans attempted to destroy it with mini-submarines and with bombs attached to driftwood.

[37] The German *Maschinengewehr* 08 or MG 08 Machine Gun; produced in a number of variants it became the standard German heavy machine gun of WWII. At the height of production Germany produced an estimated 14'400 a month.

there was fighting going on at this time about three miles away and we were sitting quiet listening to the news.

The BBC said that there was heavy fighting going on in the village of Elst and we were sitting there all quiet at that particular time, and the same again the next day. We had a laugh at that.

We were helping ourselves in regard to grub as much as we could: I went and picked enough mushrooms to do us all for breakfast one morning and the others brought some in other days. There was plenty of spuds about and fresh green vegetables in the farmhouses and they were mostly deserted so we helped ourselves.

I went down into Nijmegen every day except the day that the bridge got broken, to get water and that was another unpleasant job. Jerry was in the habit of shelling the bridge from long ranges very often and no one used to loiter in the vicinity. I used to get across it as quickly as possible although I was very lucky as there never was any shelling at the moments when I was going across, thank goodness.

I took water out one day and there was the usual shelling but we only had to take any cover on one gun site. This day was the same as all others, just the same round of sites with water, along with the same noise of shells bursting.

We rolled up at THQ and to our surprise the place was littered with wreckage and no one about. For the moment we thought that Jerry had come and driven our people away, but just as we pulled to a stop the chaps began to turn out. It appeared that Jerry had sent a salvo of six shells in a straight line and our billet was in the way of the fourth one. It hit the wall, knocking a hole in it and completely wrecked our wireless truck which was standing against the wall. What a mess it was, bits and pieces of truck and house all mixed up and strewn all around.

There was no casualties as everyone heard the familiar whistle in time to dive into the cellar. We were lucky (Phil and I) as had we arrived five minutes earlier my truck would have been in line with the wireless truck and most probably standing against it. I now began to think that God was protecting me and I still do.

We had been around Elst for twelve days now and we were told that Div was pulling out today to rest and reform, but, we were disappointed to hear that our troop were to stay on for another day, as the LAA[38] which was to relieve us would not arrive until then. The Div was being relieved by the American Airborne Div and they had not got any air cover of their own.

We did not like it but it had to be and we watched our infantry change

---

[38] Light Anti-Aircraft Regiment.

over with the Americans and then pull out. We did not feel too comfortable this night, as we did not have the same confidence in these Yanks to hold the enemy as we had in our own infantry. They were OK though and we pulled out the next day, the 6/10/44 to the accompaniment of still more shell bursts: air-bursts overhead as we flew through the village.

We got across the bridge OK and through Nijmegen to a village called Weurt. We arrived in the dark and made ourselves at home in a blacksmiths shop; we had a meal and kipped down.

The next day (Sat) I went to sites and then drew water out of the Maas Waal Canal. We stayed here again for the night and then got orders to move on the Sunday. It was lovely weather and as we were standing about, waiting to move, we watched the RAF on the way over to Germany: this was the biggest raid I had ever seen and I have seen a few; the sky was full of Lancasters for well over an hour, and I mean full. At any given moment we could see several hundred aircraft. The wireless told us the next day that there was 3000 planes on that job; what a job it must have been.

We moved down to a place called Molenhock about five miles south of Nijmegen and just outside a place called Mook. We were to only hold the enemy on this front, which was facing the Reich Waal forest, Jerry had been making some pretty strong attacks from here but we were not to attack him, only to hold him. We spent an entire month here and it was virtually a rest.

I have been a long time with this instalment but we have been knocking about quite a lot & I just couldn't get down to it.

      So long Oll & all my love
        Your ever loving
          Arth.
        XXXXXXXX

It is now 5/1/45.

Above: A German SS *Landser* involved in heavy fighting in and around the French town of Caen during the summer of 1944. He is carrying a Spandau MG 42 configured as a light support weapon, with a folding bipod and detachable drum-belt container.

Below: The Hawker Typhoon, seen here carrying rocket projectiles.

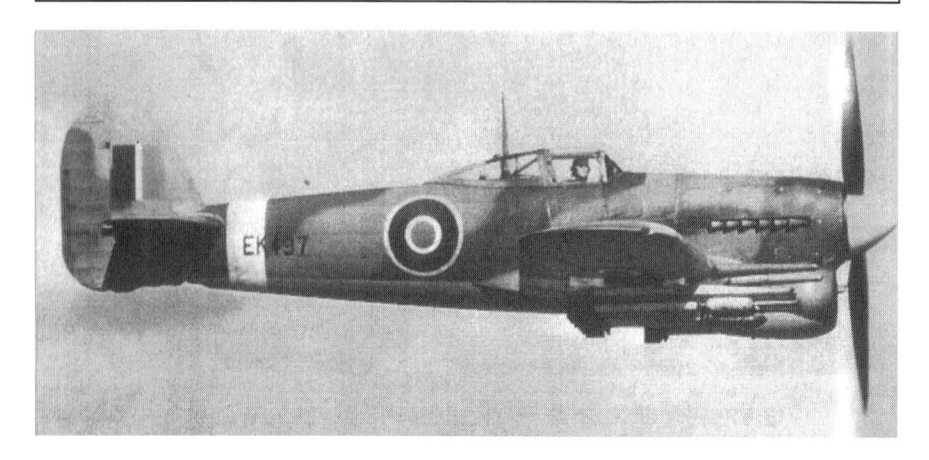

CHAPTER TEN
EPILOGUE

Unfortunately Arthur's letters end on the 5th January 1945, just over four months from the end of the war. Aided by very rough and minimal notes, Arthur was always writing three or four months after the event, and it is likely that in the final epoch of the war, when returning home was for the first time a real possibility, that the last installment did not seem worth writing. The increased tempo of the war at this stage will also be obvious to the reader from the last chapter and it is entirely possible that he simply did not find the time to write.

We do know however, from surviving notes that he and his unit continued to move with the front; the rough notes he made indicate that he travelled some distances into Holland and made return journeys to Belgium. Sadly the details of his activities there are missing. It is clear though that he made some friends whilst there, as he returned to Holland on at least two occasions after the war, with his eldest daughter Eileen, in order to visit the De Haz family. The last entry in the notes refers to his return to Hasselt in Belgium on the 3rd of March 1945. It was about this time that the Allies crossed the Rhine, encircling a significant size of the remaining German Army; on the 30th April the Reichstag was captured, Hitler committed suicide and military victory in Europe was inevitable.

Arthur's military records show that he was in North West Europe until 08th December 45. His return back to Britain was preceded by a discharge medical, and it is because of this that we know he finished the war in Mellendorf, Germany. Three months later, he was back in Britain and sent home for 76 days leave and subsequent discharge on the 22nd February 1946; his medical notes stating that he was 40 ½ years of age, fit enough for further service (although a little lighter), but with no liability for recall. It also points out that Arthur now had a scar from an old burn on the right side of his face and at some point during June 45 had been shot in the right arm, a fact that his family were not aware off, neither during the war, or after his return.

Arthur spent no less than 174 days overseas and at war, the deadliest war in human history, a war that caused an estimated 50-85 million fatalities, significantly altered geopolitics and left Europe in the grip of a crippling economic depression, establishing the foundation of the 'Cold War' that followed.

Arthur was fortunate, he returned home to his wife Olwen, a son and two daughters, the youngest of which he had left behind at six months old. The challenges of transitioning back to normality, for all the family, must have been enormous. Indeed the youngest girl, my mother, could not call this [unknown] man *"Dad"* for several years.

This book is dedicated to those who were not so fortunate.

Above: Arthur in Germany 1945.

GLOSSARY OF ABBREVIATIONS AND TERMS

Ack-ack Anti-aircraft fire, derived from the British WWII phonetic alphabet used for voice radio transmissions (AA).

Adolf Hitler Austrian-born German politician: the leader of the Nazi Party and dictator of Nazi Germany. Hitler was at the centre of World War II in Europe, and the Holocaust.

A-Echelon/A Ech Tactical grouping of vehicles and stores, to replenish and support the forward [fighting] troops.

Anti-tank Designed for use against tanks or other armoured vehicles.

Artillery Projectile–firing guns or missiles and the troops or branch of the army concerned with their use.

ATHQ Anti-Tank Headquarters.

Bailey bridge A temporary bridge formed with prefabricated, interchangeable, steel truss panels bolted together. Named after its British designer, Sir Donald Bailey.

Battalion Army unit, normally commanded by a Lieutenant Colonel and often the basic unit of tactical manoeuvre.

Battery A tactical grouping of artillery guns, the equivalent of an infantry company; consists of 3 or 4 troops.

B-Echelon/B Ech Second-line support and administrative grouping.

BHQ Battery or Brigade Headquarters.

Bivvy Bivouac: a temporary improvised encampment.

Blanco/ed A cleaning compound historically used by the British Army to whiten leather equipment.

Bofors The 40mm Morris Self-Propelled Bofors Gun.

Bombardier/Bdr	Military rank of a junior non-commission officer, specific to the Artillery. Its infantry equivalent is Corporal.
Bren Carrier	Tracked carrier-vehicle for the **Br**no **En**field machine gun.
Brigade	Army formation, usually of three battalions; deploys independently or under the command of a Division.
Caen	The main British target for the first day of the battle of Normandy. It proved a tough nut to crack and was not finally captured until 9th July 1944, by which time it was completely in ruins and virtually impassable.
Cam	Camouflage; the equipment and technique of concealing ones presence.
Captain	Commissioned (army) officer rank, commonly the second in command of a squadron.
Casevac	Military acronym for casualty evacuation from the battlefield in order to ensure prompt treatment.
Churchill	[Tank] Built by Vauxhall Motors and one of the heaviest tanks of WWII (and the basis of many specialist vehicles), the Churchill was rushed into production in the build up to the war, to protect against a German invasion.
Corps	A military formation containing two or more divisions.
CRA	Commander Royal Artillery.
Crown	British currency pre-1970. The Crown was rarely circulated, whilst the Half Crown was commonplace and worth 2 ½ shillings (30 Pennies) or 1/8th pound sterling.
Cruiser	Classification of ship intended for scouting, raiding or commerce protection. Up to 10,000 tons displacement, smaller than a battleship but larger than a destroyer.
Dakota	Douglas built transport aircraft widely utilised throughout the war for the transport of stores, personnel and the

delivery of paratroops.

Destroyer A fast and manoeuvrable warship of long-endurance, intended to escort larger vessels in a fleet, convoy or battle-group and defend them against smaller, powerful, short-range attackers.

Det Detachment: a term often used to refer to a unit assigned to different location(s) than its parent unit. Commonly a collective noun for personnel manning an artillery piece.

Div/Division A large military unit comprising of several regiments or brigades (10-30'000 men). Several divisions make up a Corps.

DR Dispatch Riders (DR) were used to deliver messages between units, a vital role in a time of limited or difficult telecommunications.

DUKW Military amphibious vehicle, the name deriving from the model naming convention of its manufacturer: D-designed in 1942, U-utility, K-all wheel drive, W-dual rear axles. The DUKWs were colloquially known as Ducks.

ENSA Entertainment National Service Administration. Established in 1939 ENSA provided entertainment for British armed forces during World War II. ENSA operated as part of the Navy, Army and Air Force Institutes (NAAFI).

Falaise Pocket An important area during the Normandy campaign in which the Allies attempted, with limited success, to trap German armour withdrawing from Normandy.

Ferdinand Tank Designed by Porsche and later renamed the *Elefant*, the Ferdinand was the first of a new breed of German tank-hunters. With enclosed crew compartment and greatly improved armour. The role of these *Jagdpanzers* (hunting tanks) was to find and destroy allied armour.

Fire Support	Direct or indirect fire from weapons such as artillery, in support of a ground force in combat.
Flying Fortress	The Boeing B-17 Flying Fortress: a US four-engine heavy bomber commonly employed in precision strategic bombing campaign of World War II, against German industrial and military targets. B17s are estimated to have dropped 640,000 tons of bombs during WWII.
Foxhole	A small and often shallow defensive fighting position.
Franc/Fr	The currency of France, Belgium and others before the introduction of the Euro in 1999. Arthur often abbreviates this in his text as Fr.
Free-Dutch	Some 1700 Dutch people managed to escape to England and offered themselves for service against the Germans. They were known as the *Engelandvaarders* (England-farers) or more colloquially as the Free-Dutch.
Frigate	Any of several types of warship, the term having been used for various roles and sizes.
Fuhrer	The self-appointed title (*leader* or *guide*) of Adolf Hitler, the leader of the German Nazi Party and Supreme Commander of the Wehrmacht.
Grenadier	Historic term retained by various military units of the Allies and Axis, demonstrating their elite or specialist pasts in the delivery of Grenades, where strength was paramount. Also used as a rank, for example a *panzer-grenadier* was the lowest rank in the German mechanized infantry, the equivalent of a British infantry Private.
Gunner/Gnr	Lowest rank in the artillery, the equivalent to an infantry Private.
Half-track	A vehicle with both tracked and wheeled propulsion.
Howitzer	A short-barrelled artillery weapon, which projects its shell on a lofted trajectory, over a relatively low velocity.

HQ	Headquarters.
Infantry	The branch of the army whose specific purpose is to engage with and fight with the enemy.
Jerry	A nickname given to Germans during the Second World War by soldiers and civilians of the Allied nations, in particular by the British.
LAA	Light Anti-Aircraft artillery.
Lancaster	British four-engine heavy bomber.
LCT	Landing Craft Tank was an amphibious assault ship for landing tanks on beachheads.
LST	Landing Ship Tank was a larger version of the LCT amphibious assault ship for landing tanks on unprepared ground. The original versions were made from altering existing ships, but by the end of the war the UK and US had manufactured more than 1000 specialist vessels.
Luftwaffe	The aerial warfare branch of the German *Wehrmacht*, the unified armed forces of wartime Germany.
Me109	German interceptor aircraft produced by Messerschmitt.
Mobile Baths	A temporary and mobile bathing service provided by the Royal Army Ordnance Corps.
MP	Military Police.
MT	Motor Transport (MT) refers to the operation and maintenance of a military vehicle fleet and sometimes to the service members who operate and maintain them.
Nazi/Nazism	Member of the National Socialist German Workers' Party/the ideology and practice associated with the Nazi Party. Nazism subordinated individuals and groups to the needs of the nation, state and leader; it was characterised by its form of fascism that incorporates racism.

OP Position (normally concealed) from where a soldier can watch enemy movements and direct fire support, such as artillery.

Panzer Grenadiers German mechanized infantry.

PIAT British anti-tank weapon: Projector Infantry Anti-tank.

Pontoon Bridge Supporting temporary bridge made up of flat bottom boats or drums.

Quart Imperial unit of volume equal to a quarter of a gallon or two pints.

RAMC Royal Army Medical Corps.

Red Cross The International Red Cross is an international humanitarian movement founded to protect human life and health, to ensure respect for all human beings, and to prevent and alleviate human suffering.

RE/Royal Engineers The Corps of Royal Engineers, commonly known as the Sappers, provides military engineering and other technical support to the British Armed Forces.

Recce Military abbreviation for reconnaissance, the act of exploring beyond the forward line of own troops.

Regt/Regiment. Military unit, normally consisting of two or more battalions. Composite part of a Brigade.

REME The corps of Royal Electrical Mechanical Engineers.

Slit Trench An extended defensive fighting position, larger than a foxhole and commonly deep enough to stand in.

SP Self-propelled.

Spandau The German Maschinengewehr 08 or MG 08 Machine Gun; produced in a number of variants it became the standard German heavy machine gun of WWII. At the height of

	production Germany produced an estimated 14'400 a month.
Spearhead	The leading force of an attack.
Strafing	The action of attacking from the air with bullets and rockets.
SS	The ☐☐☐*zstaffel*: a major paramilitary organization under Adolf Hitler. The SS grew from humble beginnings as Hitler's personal bodyguards, to be one of the most powerful and feared organizations of the Third Reich and was responsible for many war crimes.
Stag	A colloquial term referring to sentry duty. E.g. to be "☐*n*☐ *stag*".
Sten	**S**heperd and **T**urpin (**En**field UK) submachine gun.
Teller Mine	German plate (☐*eller*) shaped, pressure activated, anti-tank mine.
THQ	Troop Headquarters.
Thunderbolt	P47 interceptor aircraft.
Tiger (Tank)	German heavy tank weighing over 65 metric tons and carrying 80 rounds of ammunition. Partly due to the success of Allied bombing, less than 500 were eventually produced.
TNT	Trinitrotoluene, an explosive compound. The name however is often used to refer to any type of explosive.
Tp Com	Troop Commander.
Tp/Troop	Army unit, subordinate to a Battery; consists of two or more sub units.
Typhoon	Allied fighter-bomber produced by Hawker.
U-boat	The anglicized version of the German word U-Boot:

	German military submarines. Although efficient weapons against naval warships, they were most effectively used in economic warfare, enforcing a blockade against shipping carrying military and civilian supplies.
Wallah	Arabic, indicating a person involved in some kind of activity; a colloquial term widely used throughout the military since the time of the British Raj in India.
Wilts (The)	The Wiltshire Regiment: local soldiers recruited in and around Wiltshire.
Yanks	Short for Yankee: informal term for an American.
Yard/Yd	Imperial unit of length equal to 3 feet or 36 inches; its metric equivalent is 0.9144 metres.

GAZETTEER OF MUSEUMS

You can find out more about Arthur's war by visiting the following museums:

Imperial War Museum
Lambeth Road
London
SE1 6HZ

www.iwm.org.uk/
02074 165 000

Imperial War Museum
Duxford
Cambridge
CB22 4QR

www.iwm.org.uk/visits/iwm-duxford
01223 835 000

Firepower, The Royal Artillery Museum
Royal Arsenal
Woolwich
London
SE18 6ST

www.firepower.org.uk/
02088 557 755

National Army museum
Royal Hospital Road
Chelsea
London
SW3 4HT

www.nam.ac.uk/
02078 816 606

ABOUT THE EDITOR

Graham 'Sven' Hassall was born 6th August 1974, six weeks after Arthur's death. However, growing up in the extended family environment that he created, reminders of his presence were never far away. In particular the carpentry of wardrobes, tables and workshops that decorated the homes of his son and daughters.

Graham inherited both Arthur's affection for utility and for reading and writing, and now enjoys a growing portfolio of his own works. Graham is married to Sarah-Jane and has two sons: Owain and Evan, who enjoy their great-grandfather's legacy of hand-made wooden toys.

Printed in Great Britain
by Amazon.co.uk, Ltd.,
Marston Gate.